MW01172955

# DANGER:
# 50 THINGS YOU SHOULD
# NOT DO WITH A
# NARCISSIST

# BY

# H G TUDOR

**All Rights Reserved**

**Copyright 2015**

# Danger:

## 50 Things You Should Not Do With A Narcissist

### By

### H G Tudor

Published by Insight Books

# Dedications

This one is for you.

# Introduction

Hello and welcome to my observations about the fifty things that you should not do with a narcissist. As usual, I am providing you with the benefit of the perspective from a narcissist. This gives you a rare and advantageous view to enable you to understand how my kind and me think and behave. This will enable you to be better warned and in turn advise others that may be engaged in doing the dance with the narcissist what to be aware of. Furthermore, you may be fortunate enough to provide this information to those who have not yet had the misfortune to be ensnared by a narcissist so they can guard themselves against the inevitable pain and misery that arises from being drawn into our twisted world.

The world is becoming a dangerous place because my kind is on the increase. More than ever you need to be aware about what we do, how we behave and what you should do to protect yourselves. One in six people are narcissists. That means at a dinner party there is one already sat around the table. Is it your partner? What about your best friend? Her husband. We are there, moving freely amongst you because the world is allowing us to do this

Our kind is multiplying. Society is geared more than ever to not only creating more of our type but also providing us with so many methods by which we can ensnare you with the advance of technology.

You will be most likely aware that everyone has narcissistic tendencies and the way the world is, it is pandering to those traits, encouraging them and growing them. Competition is good. You should be better than everyone else. You have to love yourself before you can love anyone else. Put you first and everything else will fall into place. You deserve it. You are worth it. You are special.

The demand for instant gratification is fuelling this epidemic of narcissistic tendencies. There is little concept of earning a living through hard graft and application. A sense of entitlement has grown; the world owes you a living. It must be about the here and now. I do not believe in jam tomorrow, because I demand it today. Consider all of these things and how they have created an air of immediacy.

1. Fast food;
2. 24 hour supermarkets
3. On-line shopping
4. 24 hour helplines
5. On demand television programmes and films
6. Downloaded music
7. Email, text, skype, messenger.
8. Win the lottery
9. Win a talent show
10. Be famous for being famous
11. Be on a reality television show and wealth and fame will follow
12. Sue somebody for compensation; it has to be someone else's fault surely? They owe me.
13. Processed food and ready meals.

14. 24-hour banking

15. 24 hour bars and restaurants

So much is available now. So often the shortcut to wealth, beauty and fame is dangled before people causing them to want it all and somehow believe that they are the ones who are entitled to have it. People are encouraged to grab what they can because if they do not, someone else will. You snooze you lose, nobody remember who comes second, show me a good loser and I will show you a loser, eyes on the prize and so on.

This environment, which is so conducive to narcissistic tendencies, can only be a fertile breeding ground for the full-blooded narcissist. Who could function normally and healthily when they are fed a daily diet of compliance? Entire industries have sprung up based on pandering to people. Every part of your body can be changed, buffed or polished. It can be made bigger or smaller, stronger, more durable and more attractive. Why bother putting the hours in on a treadmill when you can have the fat sucked from your body? Your nose is big because your father has a big nose and his before him, but you can engage in some rhinoplasty and have it altered. The world has become more and more a selfish place with individualism lauded above everything else.

All this has done is create the potential for more people to cultivate narcissistic tendencies and thus step onto the slippery slope to becoming a full-blown narcissist. I know the experts repeatedly make mention of how narcissists are created during childhood, usually from some traumatic event, through neglect or through being deemed to be a golden child. There may be some mileage in these theories but they do not know for sure. Consider that last item, the golden child. Of course all parents believe their children are wonderful. That is a necessary pre-requisite for the parent to care, nourish and support their child, but now it has crossed over into something that is far from healthy. It is becoming the norm to treat your child as some kind of superstar even when it is patently clear they are not special in the slightest. Everyone wins a prize at sports day in school. Children are lavished with praise and fail to experience the sting of constructive criticism that will make them try harder. Society is now creating an expectation that every child is special, is capable of great things and thus should be afforded special treatment. The creation of this expectation is dangerous. Simone de Beauvoir argued in the Second Sex, amongst other things, that the maternal instinct is not actually natural but is in fact a construct of a patriarchal world. Women are expected to want to care for children because men have made them believe that is their role. Is something similar not happening with children? They are being brought up to believe they are special, that they are entitled and that they can do what they like because of their brilliance? The seeds of creating more and more narcissists are being spread.

Not only is this prevailing culture of a narcissistic cultivation creating more narcissists, it also provides ideal cover for those of us moving amongst you already. Consider this. Once upon a time someone who believed they were above everyone else, someone who was grandiose in gesture and word, uncaring and self-centred stuck out like a sore thumb. That is not so much the case today. Pause for a moment and consider amongst your family, your friends, your acquaintances and your colleagues, the people who stand in the crowd each week with you watching junior football or in the congregation at your church and ascertain which of them: -

1. Always talks about themselves;
2. Never listens;
3. Boasts about their achievements;
4. Goes missing when there is hard work to do;
5. Never shows a caring side;
6. Acts in a selfish manner;
7. Is unpunctual and/or cancels arrangements at the last minute;
8. Borrows money but never repays it;
9. Borrows items and breaks them without replacing them or never return the said item
10. Belittles other people with back-handed compliments
11. Throws temper tantrums

Chances are you know will several people who do one of more of these things. Now, I am not suggesting that he or she amounts to being a narcissist. Not at all, that falls to a more clinical analysis, but what it does show is that narcissistic tendencies prevail all around and they are increasing because of the way society is. This means that those of us who are narcissists become even harder to spot. Not only are we masters of disguise that trap you in an instant, our surroundings are being altered so that they provide us with even more concealment and cover. It has never been a better time to be a narcissist.

Against this chilling development you need as much information as you can muster to protect yourself against our devilish ways. You need to know what you should not do with us. Here are fifty instances of what you should not do with a narcissist. Read, digest and disseminate.

HG Tudor
November 2015

# 1. Become Ensnared

This does seem rather obvious but it happens time and time again. To be captured by a narcissist begins as a glorious coupling between two people who seem utterly made for one another. You did not expect this to happen. You might have known about us for some time, we may be a childhood friend or someone you knew at college. We might have been colleagues or even just began as friends on social media, bumping into one another in a chat room or a speculative friend request based on an inviting photograph. The world of Internet dating, where the narcissists of this world cast their lines, may have been proven to be the place where our paths crossed. The dangling hooks, the nets, the cages and the traps that my kind and me place all around are numerous and always camouflaged.

You drift along unaware that a red dot has just landed on your back from the laser sighting of my rifle. A target has appeared on your chest ready for my arrows of desire to be fired towards you. Your GPS co-ordinates have been entered into my computer ready to rain down those love missiles on you. You are walking through a minefield and in all likelihood you will tread on one of those mines.

I have explained in my introduction how society has changed to allow the creation of more narcissists, that the way the world is framed means that there is an explosion of narcissistic tendencies. This not only enables our kind but it also makes us harder to spot. The risk of you becoming ensnared becomes higher. It is hard enough to identify us when we come for you, when you do not have the benefit of any prior knowledge or understanding, but now the world has handed us camouflage paint and cloaking devices. You are in danger.

You are sucked into our world and made to feel wonderful. It will not last. You may be among the fortunate and manage a few years before our behaviour changes. You will be in the minority. With most it is months. We begin to devalue you and everything you once loved and relished about us is cast aside. It is painful, it is confusing and it is incomprehensible unless you have some form of guide as to what is going on. Everyone recognises what has happened when they look at it with the benefit of hindsight but when you have been sucked in and spun around so that you no longer know left from right, the very last thought that will cross your mind is that a narcissist has ensnared you. That amazing golden period was an illusion. It will be ripped away from you almost overnight in some cases. Yes, you may be given false hope by us giving you glimpses of it as we make you dance for us, but it can never be recovered because it never existed. It was never real.

Instead you will be subjected to a campaign of abuse. There is no need to call it anything else. Our behaviour towards you will be abhorrent and will encompass a vast array of manipulative techniques that we deploy in order to control and abuse you. Emotional, physical, sexual and financial atrocities will be meted out against you. You will not recognise much of it at first, as it will be delivered to you with a smile and the pouring of sugar in your ear. You will be left confused, bereft and broken. You will lose your friendships and your family. You work will suffer. Your health will deteriorate. Your finances will be wrecked and your sanity left hanging by a shred.

You will have no comprehension as to why this has happened to you and why you have been chosen because we are such skilled abusers that we make you think it is your fault. We have you believing our lies, we have you thinking that it is night when it is day and that everything you knew was wrong. We do this because with our charm and allure we coax you into a malign and warped world that we have created. It is a fantasy where we rule as king and all we care about it extracting fuel from you.

We will cheat on you, lie to you, make you weep, have you scream in frustration and still you will not go. We chain, shackle, bind and tie you to us in so many ways in order to ensure that you dance to our tune and you will not go away. We will leave you spent and broken and then return once more to pick over what is left of you in the hope of finding another droplet of fuel.

To be ensnared by a narcissist is a bewildering and terrifying ordeal. Many never fully recover. As with most things in the world, prevention is better than cure. Accordingly, never become ensnared by a narcissist. Read on and you will learn how you can avoid that happening and what you should do if we have begun to sink our claws into you.

## 2. Accept our Flattery

We are the masters of flattering to deceive. It is the method by which we draw you in to our nightmare world. We embark on our campaign of love bombing. This consists of various means of making you feel loved, wanted and desired. We pay you plenty of attention, we send you gifts and we take you to special places and events. We put you at the centre of our world and raise you up on a pedestal. As part of this love bombing, the thing we do the most of is flatter you. Words come easy to us. They are disposable tools that we can readily summon and cost us nothing to use. The cost for you however will be far higher. We engage in flattery each and every day in order to pull you towards us, to make you want us like you have never wanted anyone else before and ultimately to have you fall in love with us.

Everybody likes to be complimented, that is a natural reaction. Polite behaviour also dictates that it is deemed a good thing to offer a compliment to somebody, remarking how their new hairstyle suits them or that the fresh fragrance they are wearing is most appealing. Through our keen observation of behaviour allied with our natural ability to seek out those who have been hurt and damaged, we know the impressive power that comes by flattering somebody. It is often the case that when we come along somebody will have hurt you previously. You will be most wary of being subjected to more pain and we know that. We also know that our saccharine words will provide succour to you and override your hesitancy to become involved with someone again. The allure of our flattery will prove irresistible to you and perversely, the very fact that you are nursing some emotional wounds from a previous relationship will mean that our empty compliments will actually be more effective.

Our skill in this is heightened because we have made a study of you before we made our move to ensnare you. We have monitored you from afar, spoken to your friends and combed through your social media in order to determine what you like and what you dislike. Thus, if we have learned that you are a voracious reader of books, and then we will compliment you on how well read you are and flatter you by speaking highly of the books that we know you enjoy. Your professed interest in George Orwell means we will quote from Animal Farm and 1984. We will suggest other similar works, perhaps arriving on a date with a copy of Aldous Huxley's Brave New World for you to read. We will speak in glowing terms about how we admire those who read extensively and take an interest in literature. This, of course, will only be one of many tendrils that we extend in order to coil around you and draw you in. Absolutely anything and everything about you becomes fair game for our effusive praise.

We are invariably charming and excellent wordsmiths, finding many ways to say the same thing. Your appearance will always be remarked on, every time we see you. This will happen several times a day.

"I love how fresh-faced you are when you first wake up."

"You carry that outfit really well, I am impressed."

"You don't need a lot of make-up but the little you do use really accentuates your features well."

"I had a feeling you would have a Prada handbag; you suit that style."

All of that has been said before you have even left the house. We will find praise in anything. The car you drive, the way you write the letter 'T', the meals you make, the friends you keep and your beautiful singing voice. Each and every day we fire our flattering missiles towards you and you willingly allow them to explode over you, revelling in the pleasure you feel from our false words. These missiles will come in several forms. We will look you in the eye and whisper our compliments to you, we will pen beautiful letters and notes, leaving them under your windscreen wiper or placing them through your letterbox. Most of all however we shall use technology by sending you texts, emails and messages on social media. This near constant avalanche of flattery will become addictive to you. You will find that you are waiting for the next message to arrive. You will see your phone light up and our name appear on the front screen and feel that surge of excitement as you anticipate another slice of delight. You begin to crave our compliments. All of this is part of our careful design. We know you want to be loved and swept off your feet. We know you will respond to those overtures. We know that it will become something you come to need and expect. We know you will want us and want to be with us so that we become your sun around which you will orbit. It is a carefully orchestrated assault of false flattery and unless you are forewarned to recognise it, it works every single time.

At this early stage in our relationship you will be blown away by the incessant bombardment of praise we subject you to. How delightful to be treated this way, especially after the horrible behaviour you had to endure in your previous relationship. This feels like nirvana. Yes, it may seem a little over the top at times, after all, you know you have never won awards for the way you look and your cookery skills are proficient but hardly Michelin star quality. Yet, we are just being polite and taking an interest aren't we?

No, we have no interest in you whatsoever. All that matters to us is that we pour sugar in your ear and you become coated in it so that you fall into our trap. It may seem counter-intuitive to reject someone when they are being pleasant towards you, but reject us you must as otherwise you will become a hostage to our hunger for fuel from you. You must ensure that your default setting is to be sceptical about what somebody says to you when you first meet him or her. Train yourself to be able to recognise the over the top flow of flattery that we send in your direction.

Should you meet somebody, you should be aware of the following: -

1. Compliment after compliment after compliment is not normal;

2. Praising some trait or interest you have (when we should only know very little about you at the outset) is a matter for concern;

3. Taking an excessive interest in your interests when we hardly know you is a warning indicator;

4. Being praised for something when you know that it is not truly merited is a danger sign.

No matter how sincere we appear to be, no matter how earnest our words and how they will ring with some truth, you must not believe what we are saying to you. It is all empty flattery.

## 3. Rush into Commitment

Our purpose in life is to extract fuel from you. In order to achieve this sole aim, we need you around us and committed to us so that our source of fuel is almost always present. We do not need to be physically with you to achieve this. The readiness of technology to enable us to remain in contact with you through a plethora of methods satisfies this desire for often and repeated contact. What we need to achieve is that you feel compelled to interact with us. You must feel obliged to spend time with us, answer our telephone calls and/or respond to our text messages. Part of this is achieved by flattery as described in the previous chapter. When we send you a compliment in a text, you, being a decent and well-mannered person will answer it. Often you will write back conveying your thanks and also sending a compliment to us as well. This provides us with what we want. Your attention and admiration.

We need this obligation to become deeper however. We not only want you to respond when we get in touch with you, we also want you to contact us irrespective of our approach to you. We want you to think of us from the moment you wake up so that you call us. We require you to have us in our thoughts so that you will provide us with the attention that we crave.

Unlike a normal, healthy relationship, which develops over time at a sensible pace, which is acceptable to both people, we want to rush you into commitment. We want you attached to us a soon as possible so that you are beholden to our demands and thus you feel obligated to do what we want. If you have a serious commitment to us, we know, because you are that decent and honest person, that you will not renege on your obligations. You will get in touch to ask how we are, you will follow us from room to room to ascertain what is wrong when we subject you to a bout of silent treatment and you will do your utmost to keep us happy. We know you will do this because we recognise that as an empathic individual you take your responsibilities seriously and adhere to them. As part of a couple, you will look to maintain that state of affairs by doing anything and everything possible to ensure that we do not break up. This means that you will bend over backwards to facilitate us. Even in a normal relationship the split between two people is rarely an even fifty per cent each. Often one person does more for the other and sometimes this percentage vacillates dependent on the particular strand of the relationship. On the one hand, one person may contribute more financially than their partner but then that person provides more in terms of handling the household's administrative affairs. There is nothing wrong with one person giving more than the other in a relationship. In relationships involving my kind and me however that percentage is so heavily skewed in our favour, across all elements of the relationship that is bordering on indentured servitude. It has to be this way in order for us to extract the fuel we need. We do not like to expend our own energy in maintaining the relationship. We prefer to use it to acquire more fuel, either by hunting out new sources of supply or by unleashing our wide variety of manipulative wiles against you. Thus, in order to conserve our fuel for our malign purposes, it falls to you to expend your energies in the upkeep of our relationship.

The extent and degree by which we require you to give your all, often for little in return, means that in the early stages of a relationship most people would regard that as wrong and seek to remove themselves from this unpleasant position. We cannot have you do that. We will use flattery to keep you where we want you but we are unable to maintain this for too long, as it will take up too much of our energies. Accordingly, we need to make you commit to us in some other form. This means we will look to achieve one of the following:

1. Move in together (usually we prefer to move into your home whilst keeping our own property as a bolthole, which we can remove ourselves to when we are subjecting you to silent treatment. Also, we like to move into your property as this enables us to argue that you should shoulder the bills, since after all, it is *your* house.)

2. Get engaged and married; and/or

3. Get you pregnant or become pregnant

By achieving one or all of these situations we are able to bind you to us. You will think that this is wonderful. We are evidently so in love with you that we want to take such a major step with you. It has nothing to do with love, it is all about ensuring that you are committed to us and thus in the best possible position to provide us with fuel. By bringing about these scenarios you are less likely to leave and more likely to want to keep trying to please us, even when we are subjecting you to awful devaluation. You do not want to give up since you are, for example, a firm believer in the institution of marriage. You try to keep us together because your parents have always been together and you always swore you would do the same. You want to overcome the problems (always caused by us, not you, despite what we keep telling you) because we have children together and you do not want them to come from a broken home. All your ingrained values are the methods by which we know that you will not shirk your responsibilities and by which you will remain committed to us.

It also provides the means by which we can seek to hoover you back in at a later stage after we have discarded you but decide we want to, we have to, extract some further fuel from you. Consider these statements: -

"I decided to give her a further chance; she is still my wife after all."

"I know what he did was wrong but he said he is sorry and he wants to be there for our children. I cannot deny them that can I?"

"He cannot go back to that dingy apartment and be on his own. I don't like to think of him sat alone, not when it is clear there is something wrong. This is our home and he should be here."

Any of those sound familiar?

We will move at light speed to bring about this level of commitment. We make you think that this is the ultimate in showing our commitment to you. That is wrong. It is all about making your committed to us. We do not recognise that we have any obligation to you at all. Nobody can know one another well enough to marry after six weeks. What trials and tribulations have you experienced together to ensure that you are compatible? What situations have you seen one another in to know that your relationship can endure the slings and arrows that life will send your way? We however will blind you to all of this with our campaign of love bombing so that you will seize this chance to bond with us in the ultimate fashion, in an instant. You will not want to lose somebody as marvellous as us, someone who has treated you better and more wonderfully than anyone else. You will do anything to keep us and the fact that we have suggested that we move in together has made your dreams come true. He must feel the way I do if he is proposing so soon, mustn't he?

Once the commitment has been achieved you will see our behaviour towards you alter. Sometimes it is almost over night, sometimes it is months, or maybe if you are really lucky (or is that unlucky?) it will be a few years, but that change will come. The fact we have secured your commitment provides us with carte blanche to do as we please and you will put up with it. In fact, the existence of this commitment means that you will allow yourself to be subjected to the very worst of our behaviour and you will work harder to try and make things right.

The knockout blow in terms of securing commitment is to have children with you. This is a very powerful method of ensuring we get what we want. Not only will you be loath to have the relationship end, for the sake of the children, should you muster sufficient strength and willpower to escape us, the fact we will still be able to see the children means you can never be truly free of our influence. We will have a conduit by which we can continue to exert our behaviours over you and extract fuel from you. This may be by virtue of contact with you (speaking on the telephone about arrangements concerning the children or attending in person to collect or drop them off). It may also be by using the children as a method by which we triangulate with you. We secure their affections by denigrating you and thus prompting you to react when the children repeat our lies about you. Your only hope is that eventually the children see through our façade and decide they do not want to have anything to do with us. That is unlikely to happen (if at all) for a number of years. You also run the real risk that our behaviours will have created another version of ourselves in one of our children and thus the nightmare will be propagated.

Do not make any of these commitments with one of our kind. If someone is rushing you towards any one or all of these commitments, you are being rushed towards the gates of hell. Turn around and run in the other direction.

## 4  Financial Commitments

Do not enter into any financial commitments with my kind and me. It will only ever lead to financial devastation. No matter how hard that we persuade you to enter into joint financial commitments, lend us money or support us, resist it. It will only end in considerable stress and concern for you. We are notorious disaster areas in matters of money. This is because we either have plenty of money but have no concept of using our resources for your benefit. It belongs to us and therefore should be used for us only. Alternatively, we have no money (although we will of course pretend to the contrary in order to seduce you) and we are entitled to be supported by you. Not only will we drain you of your financial resources we will also leave you with further financial woes owing to our behaviour.

Four matters drive how we behave with you in a financial sense.

1. Our massive sense of entitlement;

2. Our grandiose view of ourselves;

3. We do not recognise boundaries; and

4. We want you bound to us.

Our overwhelming sense of entitlement means that we have a particularly skewed view of financial arrangements. What we earn belongs to us and is only ever used to demonstrate how brilliant we are and how you are inferior. Look at how much I earn, observe how splendid my car is and admire my extensive wardrobe. We do not believe in sharing, unless it is you doing the sharing. Of course, we have already blindsided you into thinking that we are the epitome of generosity by showering you with gifts and treating you to expensive city breaks or spa treatments at country retreats during our love bombing of you. All of this was designed to lure you into our web. It was also done to make you think that we are generous. Furthermore, it provides us with a stick to beat you with at a later stage.

"I cannot believe you are asking me to contribute to the bills after all the things I have bought for you."

"I do need you to lend me that money, after all, I have spent plenty on you haven't I?"

We believe that we should be afforded special treatment. You should pay for the drinks every time we are out, friends should pick up the restaurant bill since I gave them a little piece of advice, that wallet I found in the street with money now belongs to me (they must have been an idiot to drop it and thus do not deserve to have that money). I don't have to pay that fine, as I should not have been given a ticket in the first place. I under declare my liability for taxation because I create wealth through my company. Why should I have to pay all those taxes when I am generating income for these people and they are thus paying tax? Why on earth should I pay you maintenance when you decided to divorce me?

Our grandiose view of ourselves means that we love to make a show of spending money. We will pick up the bar tab for everybody on a night out (and then process it through expenses by pretending that it was a business cost) or we will choose the most expensive vehicle which means we won't have enough to pay child support, but that does not matter, so long as we can show off in that new convertible.

The failure that is inherent in our make up to recognise boundaries means that we treat everyone else's possessions as belonging to us. In the most minor form this presents itself as domestic theft. You have baked some cookies to sell at a charity event and you have told us that is why they have been made. We will still eat them because we were hungry and why shouldn't we have those cookies? We will find any reason to justify this boundary transgression.

"I was hungry and you hadn't left me anything else to eat. What was I expected to do? Starve?"

"Well I do contribute to this household so half of them did belong to me."

"You really wouldn't get so worked up about some cookies if you really loved me, would you?"

"I cannot believe you are making such a fuss about a few cookies, not after everything I have done for you."

We are justified in our action. This justification permeates from the minor to the major in terms of our stampeding all over your financial position. The type of financial misconduct that we will engage in may include: -

1. Using your credit card to pay for things for ourselves;

2. Using your credit card to take other women/men out and/or buy them gifts;

3. Taking out loans in your name;

4. Re-mortgaging the property without your consent;

5. Stealing money from your purse/wallet and bank account;

6. Emotionally blackmailing you to ensure family members loan me money;

7. Expecting you to be the bread winner whilst we do nothing;

8. Expecting a far greater contribution from you to the household than proportionate to our respective incomes;

9. Putting all the household bills in your name so we can evade responsibility for them

10. Failing to pay bills and then expecting you to bail out the position

As with the previous chapter we will be rushing to ensure you have a financial commitment with us. You will regard this as a desirable statement of intent on our part. We regard it as just another tendril that we can wrap around you to keep you close and then later provide us with a method of generating reactions from you.

We always walk away from any carnage that we create. That is one of our key attributes. You will be the one left with the debts and a shattered credit rating. You will lose the house and your possessions as you realise I have defaulted on the loans that I secured against your property and possessions. You will find that I will not repay the money that you lent me and in some cases of my kind, there is little point in taking legal action to recover it. I probably had little money to begin with and what I did have has been spent on the various addictions that my kind often have. If I am a viable financial target I will try and grind you down through a war of attrition by making you spend more than you might reasonably recover, by hiding my assets and not declaring them. Remember, I am a pathological liar so it will not trouble me in any way to engage in deceitful conduct in order to prevent you from recovering money from me or getting me to pay in order to fulfil my obligations to you and our children. It will be an exhausting excursion trying to obtain money from me and of course I will revel in making you dance for me with my false promises of repayment as I continue my manipulation of you to obtain even more fuel from you.

Do not become financially entwined with my kind and me. Ever.

# 5  Integrate with Your Networks

Continuing the theme of creating the ties that bind, I will look to integrate into your various networks. We want to know who your friends are, we need to meet your family and ascertain who your colleagues are. As usual, we will do all of this under the auspices of wanting to get to know everything about you because we love you so much. We do of course want to know everything about you, but we only want to do that in order to enable us to use that information for our purposes and against you. Our key aims in placing ourselves within your social and familial networks are as follows: -

1.  To gather information about you;

2.  Identify ideal candidates for the creation of Lieutenants;

3.  Generate further sources of fuel;

4.  Effect our manipulative techniques;

5.  Isolate you; and

6.  Bind you closer to us.

Your networks will provide us with plenty of information about you. As ever, we shall place our mask of charm across our face and have your friends and family think we are delightful in wanting to know more about you. They will offer this information up without hesitation. They will have no reason to think that it is being harvested for an ulterior motive. Indeed, it is unlikely that they have even recognised what I am. Your well-meaning friends will furnish me with knowledge about past relationships thinking they are laying down a marker to me as to how I should ensure I treat you correctly. In reality, I want this information to know which barbed remarks I can throw your way in due course. Your family will gently tease you about some childhood indiscretion, which I will recognise as actually being a catalyst for something deeper. I will sniff around this off the cuff anecdote as I garner more about what really happened and how it has affected you. Knowing about your childhood enables me to deploy some powerful denigrating techniques. Anything I can say or do which propels you back to feeling like a helpless and pathetic child is weapons grade material in my armoury. So often your parents or siblings, or a great auntie will recount that tale about how you soiled yourself in school. What they have not realised is that you did that because you were terrified of the large spider in the school toilets and that was why you did not relieve yourself in time. A former school friend has filled in the gaps in this supposedly amusing event. My occasional rendition of "incy wincy spider" has its desired effect in making you feel small and embarrassed again.

I need to post my Lieutenants to enable my manipulation of you to be effective. I of course have several drawn from my ranks, my friends, my contacts and colleagues. The most potent ones however are those, which I have recruited from your side. Not only will they provide me with regular pieces of information about you, either from your past and/or what you have been doing recently, they are brainwashed to support my stance and reject yours. The way in which I always know where you have been is something I will use to cross-examine about you and accuse you of lying, to cover up my own behaviours. I absolutely adore the way that a converted Lieutenant leaves you crestfallen as you try to convince them that I have been the one who has behaved horrendously. The Lieutenant will have been primed to side with me and pour scorn on your protestations. This leaves you confused and doubting yourself.

As you have become aware, my kind and I are creatures of duplicity. To the outside world we are charming pleasant and successful. Behind the closed front door, the mask comes off and the beast within is unleashed. This public face makes us immensely popular with your social and familial networks.

"Oh yes, please bring HG he is the life and soul of the party."

"You and HG must come for dinner. All the family will be there. We are delighted you have met someone who looks after you so well."

"Make sure you invite HG to drinks, he is hilarious."

Not only does this mean I have a coterie of admirers providing with the attentive fuel that I crave, they are also unlikely to accept your tales of woe when I start my devaluation of you.

"But he is always so polite when he comes to dinner."

"Are you sure? I have always found him to be so pleasant and charming."

"No, I don't think that can be right. He only ever speaks highly of you. Perhaps you misheard what he said?"

Planting myself amidst your networks enables me to be praised and admired by your parents; it allows me access to pursue your sister and then your best friend as even greater sources of supply. They will submit to my charm but will be unlikely to expose the infidelity for fear of hurting you and losing their relationship with you. I am seen as that great guy with your colleagues and the members of your club or association and I feel myself growing strong and powerful with all these supply lines being generated from those around you.

You may be aware from my writings in **Manipulated** of the variety of controlling techniques that I deploy in furtherance of my aims. Key to achieving these is the necessity of integrating myself into your networks. This allows me to create the Lieutenants that I have already mentioned, but also to use people to triangulate with you. We will learn about your close friendships with others so we can use that when we project onto you by accusing you of infidelity with certain friends. Getting amidst your friendships and connections is a fantastic method of beginning or exacerbating a number of my manipulative machinations.

Over time we will look to isolate you from these networks. Accordingly, we need to know what these relationships are in order to then move you away from them. By placing ourselves at the heart of your networks we can then interrupt them. We will aim to keep you apart from friends and family, ensuring you do not meet or speak in case this undoes the lies that we have told to you and to them. We will turn down invitations from those who wish to see you so that eventually they give up asking. We will persuade you that your family do not care and that your so-called friends have been saying things about you, so that you prefer to spend time with me and do not bother with them. All of this is carefully orchestrated so that your position is weakened and that you become fully immersed in the false reality that I have created for you.

Finally, this step is designed (as with many of the things I do) to bind you closer to me. This works in two ways. Initially, by seeing me getting on so well with the people that you care about, you will admire me all the more and be delighted that I have become friends with your friends so easily and that I have been welcomed into your family with open arms. Your love and admiration will increase because I have eased into these networks with such readiness. This draws you closer to me. Over time, as I seek to isolate you, this causes you to cling more tightly to me as I am your only outlet, all others having been denied to you or withdrawn by irritated friends who are tired of calling you and never getting an answer or a call back.

By allowing me into your networks you allow me to unlock my further wiles to enable me to control you and extract more fuel. You are also kissing goodbye to all those relationships, as eventually I will destroy them. Don't let me into them in the first place.

# 6  Share Your Weaknesses

From the very outset we will be mining you for information. Yes, we will have undertaken a considerable amount of research before we met you, either from those around you or from your large footprint on social media. That only provides us with enough to put a foot in the door to begin our seduction of you. We need more information and the way to do this is to spend as much time as we possibly can with you, through our love bombing of you. The gold dust of this information however is getting to know what your weaknesses are.

Our ability to sniff out damaged people serves us particularly well in this regard. The very fact that you have suffered some form of emotional damage means that you have plenty of weaknesses and vulnerabilities to divulge. We are experts at mimicry. We know how to sound concerned about somebody, even though we have no concept of how to be concerned. We cultivate trust through our application of our learned behaviours and our use of evocative language. Bear in mind as well that since we have wounded many people already we are fully familiar in the ways by which people are hurt. Is it not the case that the police turn to criminals to help them solve a particular crime? The perpetrator is the best equipped to speak of the damage that they cause. Since we dole out harm left, right and centre, we are the best placed to create a faux empathy in saying to you that we understand what it must be like for you have to suffered in this way. We do not know how it feels at all. We do know how it is executed though and this knowledge enables us to ask exactly the right questions and pretend we understand just how you feel, in order for you to open up further to us.

This sham façade of caring about you again draws you to us. We appear caring and thoughtful. We may even pretend that we have been treated in a similar fashion in order to create a bonding between us forged from an apparent mutual mistreatment. Such is our chameleon-like character that we are easily able to project an image of being hurt. After all, we do like to play the victim card too. We appear sensitive, insightful and understanding. It feels so good to be able to speak to somebody who understands. We talk of our connection and bonds, trotting out the old favourites of: -

"We are soulmates."

"We understand one another. Nobody has been able to do that before."

"It is like God has seen we have both been hurt and put us together as we deserve happiness."

Spurred on and encouraged by such platitudes you soon trust us. This is also done in conjunction with our other manipulative wiles to generate an image of longevity and deep-seated love for you. I am the one. At long last, after all that hurt, you have found me. It means you will pour out your soul to me. Each and every fear you have you want to share with me. You want me to know everything that troubles you, the bad things that have happened in the past, the matters that make you feel vulnerable, and the past events which have scarred you and the myriad of foibles and flaws which make up who you are. Like a prisoner being forced to confess, it all spills from your lips and I lap it up with huge enthusiasm. Being able to unload to me in this fashion makes you feel safe and loved and accordingly binds you closer to me. What you have also done is replenish my arsenal in readiness for me unleashing it against you.

Now I know your weaknesses. Nothing has been spared. The totality of this confession will now come back to haunt you. I will exhibit astonishing powers of recall as I use this information against you. I know you dread the dark so I will remove the light bulb and replace it with a dud one when you stay at my house. In the night I will steal out of the bedroom and then make a noise awakening you. You call out for me but there is no reply. You fumble for the light switch and to no avail. It does not take long before you are sobbing with fear and I return the champion come to save you. You told me about how you were bullied at school and that has made you shy in certain social situations. I will harness that knowledge to bully you once again, demanding that you speak up at functions and that you contribute to discussions when you would much rather sit and listen when you are with people you have first met. Naturally, the conniving nature of my control will mean that I use the weaknesses to hurt you whilst pretending I have your best interests at heart. I left you in the dark as I was preparing a surprise for you in the morning (the surprise does not appear because of course I had to come and comfort you because you were upset). I encourage you to speak up at parties so you feel involved and you get to know my friends so you build confidence. My persuasive nature has you believing these lies when the reality is that I have been plotting against you.

Those character flaws that you have divulged to me, which I assured you, were purely endearing quirks; I will now fling at you as insults. Not only will my words be hurtful and wounding it will lead to confusion, as you cannot now understand how I find those admissions annoying. I will leak your weaknesses to others in order for you to be subjected to gossip and ridicule.

We are the masters at denigrating people and you have just handed to us a fully stocked armoury which we can unleash against you whenever it suits us. This betrayal of trust is wounding yet we know, as the empathic individual that you are, you will only blame yourself. Firstly, you will scold yourself for having that weakness in the first place and then secondly you will chastise yourself for having revealed it. Rarely will you direct your anger at us. We will use this vast library of information to manipulate you, applying this knowledge to the array of techniques we use to control you.

You ought to keep your own counsel about those matters, which reveal your weaknesses and vulnerabilities. Do not release them within a moment of engaging with someone new, chances are, he or she is one of our kind and is ready to use it all against you.

## 7 Ignore Yours Instincts

I have heard it many times that the victims of our machinations have often commented,

"I thought something was not quite right in the way he kept calling me, but I ignored my instinct."

"She did seem to fall in love with me really quickly at the time and I had a feeling in my gut that this seemed a bit strange, but I just thought that that was her being passionate about me."

"I wish I had listened to my first instincts, I kept thinking something did not add up about him but I could not put my finger on what it was. It was just a feeling but I know now it was the right one."

As the type of person that is ideal prey to my kind and me, you actually exhibit a peculiar dichotomy. You are particularly attuned to the feelings of others and also your own. Accordingly, you are better placed than most to pick up on something not feeling right. I have little doubt that if you asked every victim of a narcissist they would admit that they had a gut instinct that something was not quite right but they ignored it. Those who do not fall victim to the machinations of my kind and me are rarely those that are forewarned (since few people know about a narcissist and his or her behaviour without having been exposed to it first) but those who listened to their instinct and walked away or of course there are those who are not attracted to our kind to begin with.

That is the peculiarity with how people become ensnared by my kind and me. We act in a very similar fashion. This is because we are forged in circumstances, which wire us in a particular way, and consequently this causes us to act in a similar way. We engage with a victim using barely distinguishable methods of seduction. The way we then devalue you is frighteningly similar. Yes, there are variations on a theme and there are differences in the degree of nastiness that we deploy to achieve this devaluation, but the techniques are recognisable time and time again. Ultimately, we will, as predictable in our actions as the way we have seduced and devalued, discard you; only to then try and suck you back in again at a later stage. What will cause the difference is not we, but you. It is the people we engage with that make the difference.

Essentially these people fall into four groups. The first and the rarest are those who have been burned by a narcissist before AND know they have been burned. Accordingly, they are fully aware of what we are. Some fall prey again but there are those who conform to the old adage of once bitten twice shy.

The second group are those who are not attractive to us and therefore we do not go near them. This will include other narcissists and most likely people who may not be full-blown narcissists but those who exhibit a degree of narcissistic behaviour. They are too inward looking and accordingly will not give us the fuel we crave. We are experts at spotting what people are. Accordingly, we recognise this group and do not bother making any attempt to ensnare them, as it will fail.

The third group are those that are attractive to us and thus we begin our seduction. This group however usually manages a lucky break. They may just listen to their gut instinct and walk away (although this is rare) or they may prove to be the beneficiary of some timely advice from a friend or family member who has identified what we are. The intended victim actually listens and thus has a near miss, being steered away from us before we can cast our net over them. Alternatively, circumstance conspires against us so that the intended victim moves away or becomes involved with someone else and thus our love bombs miss their target.

The final group contains the empaths. Those who have no idea what we are. Those who have no idea that they have been targeted and have no appreciation of the hell that is about to be unleashed against them. It is of course from this group that we draw our fuel and exact our damaging behaviour

Those who listen to their instincts are unlikely to have known that they have just had a brush with a narcissist. Instead they will just chalk it down to something being unusual, odd or just plain weird and they did not want anything to do with that person. You will also detect that something is not right but you invariably ignore it and make an excuse in order to diminish your concern. This is a classic reaction of the empathic individual. You like to find good in everybody and would rather think well of somebody even when it may lead to you suffering in some way. As a consequence, you will look to all the good things that we have said and done and decide that this outweighs your concern. You will persuade yourself that your instinct is really only of a minor concern when compared with everything else. Such a response is a measured one and the mark of a reasonable person but when dealing with us it is a dangerous conclusion to reach.

What you would do well to keep in mind is that we are the masters of messing with the mind. We capture your heart but we ensure that it is your reason that we keep a hold of as well. We need to do that so you will listen to what appears to be logic and reason rather than what you actually feel. We cannot master feelings. The few feelings that we do have are all based on negativity – anger, envy, hatred and jealousy. You are the ones who are in tune with your feelings and whilst we can ensnare your heart, we are not able to manipulate your inner sense as we can with your thoughts. Accordingly, although your head may be rubbishing the sensation that you feel and our words have gotten a grip on your thoughts, do not ignore your instinct. It is the one truth that you can grasp in this whirlwind of fallacy.

## 8 Ignore the Views of Others

We don't like you to listen to other people. Part of that is because we want your attention focussed on us and not someone else. Your spotlight needs to be shining on us all the time. In addition, we fear that others may work us out and brief against us in order to free you from our grasp. As I often mention, we are creatures that prefer to conserve our energy and ensure that is can be directed for the most part, if not solely, to the acquisition of fuel. If we are forced to use this energy to deal with those interfering in our carefully constructed campaigns this drains us and becomes a matter of irritation.

It is our intention to create a maelstrom of emotion and drag you into it. At first this is a whirlwind of delight and then a tornado of viciousness. What matters is that there is always a storm raging around you. When there is you are not able to see what is actually happening to you. You are incapable of processing the reality and this enables me to control you. There is no objective viewpoint that you can adopt. Annoyingly, those who are watching from the sidelines can see clearly what is happening. Their position will be one of two: -

1. They are aware of how a narcissist behaves and recognise exactly what we are; or

2. They may not be aware that a narcissist is in full effect but they recognise unusual (during the seduction phase) or abusive (during the devaluation phase) behaviour.

We also know when people are on to us. We recognise the behaviours when someone has worked out that our behaviour is untoward. This pains us greatly as it means we need to move to neutralise the effect of this person and expend energy. It will necessitate us isolating you from them and either undertaking a character assassination of you by proxy (telling you that they are saying unpleasant things about you) or engaging in a character assassination in reverse, by attacking the friend or family member who has become a threat. I am pleased to report that our manipulation of you is invariably successful. Your fear of losing us means that you are usually inclined to believe us rather than the concerned friend or family member or colleague. We are able to exert our control over you to have you believe that this person is a trouble maker, that they are jealous of your happiness or that they have done something bad (made a pass at me, said something unpleasant about you) in order to cause you to accept what we say and not them.

Experience also tells me that in this battle, my kind always wins. The friend or family member lacks the indefatigable spirit that is needed to defeat our machinations. They give up too quickly, shrugging their shoulders as they walk away saying,

"I tried but you wouldn't listen"

"I will only end up saying I told you so."

"On your head be it."

"I have tried to help but you are under his/her spell."

How many times in relationships do people choose their other half over friends and family? Nine times out of ten I will wager. This is driven by a fear of loss, the fear of being alone and also of having let something crumble to dust. You would rather sacrifice the friendship than lose that special person. That happens in normal circumstances. When we have coiled our tendrils around a victim, they always choose us over the well-intentioned friend. We make sure of it.

However, if you did actually listen to that third party you would realise (as you will eventually but when it is far too late) that he or she was right. They can see clearly what is happening. You cannot. They may have been on the receiving end of a narcissist's behaviour in the past and thus are in an excellent position to advise you. Ironically, they will show you the evidence of the malicious and abhorrent behaviour and you will deny it. You will make excuses for it and try and push it to one side. You will find that when you do wake up and realise you are being abused and you try to show us the error of our ways, you will find us making the excuses you made and being similarly in denial.

Should you be fortunate enough to have a third party draw our behaviour to your attention, question why would your friend or family member do this? Of course, we will invent reasons to try and undermine them but consider this. If you went to obtain legal advice from a lawyer, would you prefer to receive it from someone who has just qualified or someone who has practised law for twenty years? The latter naturally. Why then do you prefer to listen to someone who has only just arrived on the scene over a longstanding friend? Why are you paying heed to Johnny come lately when your parents have looked out for you from the moment you were born? Why is it in sports matches that the coach or manager is positioned on the edge of the field of play at the centre point, rather than being in the middle of all the action? The reason of course is that they obtain a far better view of what is going on from being on the touchline. Their sense of perspective is improved. Artists stand back to admire their work, so they can appreciate the big picture.

When that concerned individual takes you to one side and raises certain things with you about the way you are being treated, listen to them. They know what they are talking about.

# 9 Ignore Red Flags

In the initial stages of your encounter with my kind and me there will be the repeated fluttering of the red flags that are being hoisted. These scarlet warning signs are often lost on you. You cannot hear them, as your ears are full of the poisonous sugar that I have poured into them. You cannot see the flags because the disorientating fog that has spouted from my mouth obscures them from your view. People will talk at length about these red flags and the many forms in which they come. With much of our behaviours, you do not realise what it is until after the event and most of the time after you have received the wisdom of someone who has done the dance with a narcissist or a professional who treats those who have been victims. With the red flags however you actually do see them and you also know what has caused them. Unfortunately for you, you are either persuaded by me not to pay them any attention or you amazingly dissuade yourself that it is not worth bothering about

Whilst this "Must not" is akin to ignoring your instinct, this is more specific. With your instinct it is invariably a general, amorphous sensation that all is not right. You have a strange feeling that there is something untoward but you are unable to articulate precisely what it is. With red flags, the situation is different. In this instance, you know what it is that is wrong. You know what has been said does not ring true or you see certain behaviour and know what it is wrong. What are those red flags? Interestingly, they are numerous and as with many things about your dance with my kind and me, when you look back with the benefit of hindsight you will see more red flags than those that fly outside the United Nations building in New York. These red flags appear throughout the whole relationship with me, but those, which you need to pay greatest, heed to are the ones, which appear at the outset so that you may have a chance of escaping our clutches. They are too numerous to detail in this publication, but you can learn far more about the words and behaviour that my kind and me use which amount to red flags in my book **Evil.** Some of the early red flags however include: -

1. Premature declarations of love;

2. Incessant contact in person, through telephone calls and other media;

3. Vagueness when discussing family;

4. Vagueness when discussing past relationships;

5. Outlandish boasts;

6. Grand gestures (extravagant gifts, expensive holidays);

7. Moving the relationship forward too quickly;

8. Limited friends; and

9. A lack of corroboration about status and achievements.

Of course there are many more but these are some of the most frequent and most obvious at the outset of your interaction with one of my kind. You will easily identify them, as most of them are hardly subtle in nature.

We do our best to obscure these red flags but we are never able to avoid them being hoisted in the first place. As I have written above, we desire getting you to commit to us as soon as is possible and consequently at a far earlier stage than is natural or appropriate. We have to do this to bind you to us and this is a definite red flag. It is unavoidable that it will be raised. We hope that you will not notice it, as you will be blinded by your love for us and by our love bombing. If you happen to notice it from the corner of your eye, you may question the step with us and we will then lay on our charm in order to persuade you that it is the right thing to do and that your fears are unfounded. We are brilliant at removing your concerns. Again, we know that being the person that you are, you are likely to give us the benefit of the doubt and we play on that fact.

The red flags will always crop up. They are a necessary consequence of our unusual behaviour. You need to know what those red flags are and most important of all pay attention to them when they have been hoisted. You do not have the excuse of it being a vague feeling, instead it will be staring you in the face. You will have to deal with our silver tongue as we try to persuade you to ignore this warning, but that red flag is flying for a very good reason. Take heed of it.

## 10 Reason with Us

This is a futile exercise. Our sense of entitlement means that we are always right and you are always wrong. We may not be correct, but we are right. It is absolutely fundamental to us that we are right. It is through the adoption of this position that we maintain and reinforce our superiority. We are superior to others and we cannot countenance anything that suggests to the contrary. What you are doing when you are trying to reason with us is that you are trying to prove that we are wrong. That is not acceptable.

We look down on everybody else. We occupy a lofty and elevated position and we do not take kindly to anybody interfering with that state of affairs. By the same token, you are inferior to us. If you are trying to reason with us, you are suggesting that you are better than us. That offends us. It also drives us to anger that someone as useless as you have the audacity to try and put someone as brilliant as us straight. How dare you do that? We are also filled with horror. If we allow you to prevail in this argument or discussion, we have allowed this pathetic, useless individual to triumph over us. If that has happened, what have we become? This will often provide us with an unwelcome reminder of the beast that lurks within. The beast we have to keep shut away by garnering massive amounts of fuel to maintain our sense of power and banish any suggestion of weakness.

In order to prevent any reminder of the existence of this awful beast and also to obtain the fuel that we have to have, we cannot allow reason to prevail. It is anathema to us and if you try to draw us into a world that is predicated on logic and sense, we will resist you with a significant fury. We will fight to avoid heading down that path and instead we will aim to ensure we remain in the realm of emotion, argument and discord.

You may believe that you are not apportioning any blame when you are having this discussion with us. You adopt neutral language in order to discuss the situation rather than pointing the finger at us. That may well be the way you regard the conversation but we never do. If you are not doing what we want, you are challenging us. If you are not with us, you are therefore against us. Everything is black and white with us. We do not recognise grey and we do not recognise any attempt, which tries to show us a different outcome or course to the one that we want.

If you present some independent evidence that supports your position and thus (in our minds) must detract from ours, we will not accept it. We fail to focus on the facts, as we prefer to deal in emotion. Emotion for us equates to fuel. We want to hear you getting irritated. We want you to get annoyed, we want your voice to rise and see the tears of frustration welling in your eyes. When we see this we know we have caused this and this makes us feel powerful. If we engaged in facts, the emotion would be dissipated. If we entertained a factual argument, then we will lose the discussion and this offends us on two levels. You have dented our innate superiority and the supply of emotion and thus fuel has been cut off. We must not allow this to happen and as a consequence we will do anything we can to preserve our superiority and keep the fuel flowing.

When you try and reason with us, you are on a hiding to nothing. Since we must keep the argument going, reason is cast asunder. You keep fetching it and bringing it back and we will keep throwing it away. We follow a predictable pattern in trying to defeat your attempt to rely on reason. This methodology will always be applied in our quest to maintain the upper hand.

1. Denial;

2. Projection; and

3. Rage

You will explain to us your stance on whatever particular matter it is. We might even agree in our minds with what you have said but that does not generate any fuel for us so instead we decide to adopt a contrary stance Often however, we do not agree with you because what you are saying is not what we want and moreover we regard it as an attack against us. In these circumstances we will deny what you have accused us of or deny that state of affairs that you are relying on. Should you produce some form of independent corroboration we will deny that by attacking it. If, for example, it is a text message we will suggest you have manufactured the text (because this is the type of thing we would do). Should someone else provide a witness account we will accuse him or her of bias or that they have misheard. Should the evidence come in documentary form we will belittle it by saying it has been recorded incorrectly and even go so far as to destroy it if we can get our hands on it Once that has been done we will deny the document even existed. This will infuriate you and cause you to give us the emotional response we seek.

We will then move on to projection. In order to deflect from our weakened position in the discussion or argument, we will accuse you of some kind of conduct to shift the focus of the discussion. Invariably, we will have made up this accusation but we will repeat it as if it is gospel truth, driving the point at you over and over again as we seek to put you on the back foot and thus enable us to regain our natural superiority. Our lies and accusations know no bounds, all that matters is that you fall for this ruse and you lose sight of what has been discussed and you instead turn to defending yourself against the accusations we now level at you. This is just what we want. We want you indignant and incredulous because then you are having to debate the issue on our terms, in a heightened emotional state.

Finally, if you are still managing to press your point without recourse to emotion and you remain focussed on logic, we will unleash our rage. We will hurl insults at you, scream, shout and smash things up. Some of my kind will even resort to violence. We cannot win the argument through logic but in our minds we win by losing our tempers. This will cause you to shout and scream in return (marvellous – an emotional response), cry (wonderful – an emotional response) or storm off (hurrah – an emotional response). Even if you maintain your temper and composure and bring the discussion to a conclusion and walk away we will regard this as us having won and thus we reign supreme.

Accordingly, it is impossible to reason with us. We know you love to do this because you are programmed to be truthful and you also want everyone else to be in agreement based on the facts that have been placed before everyone. You find it astonishing that someone as intelligent as us cannot grasp the point you are making. We cannot grasp it because we do not want to. We are incapable of doing so because engaging in reason does not give us what we want. It does not provide us with the fuel that we need.

If you try and reason with us you will find it frustrating, pointless and ultimately it may even prove to be dangerous for you. I often mention that you would find it more productive to bang your head against a brick wall than try and reason with my kind and me. It is true. You will have an overwhelming desire to try and reason with us. You must resist this. We are not creatures of reason and nor will we ever be.

## 11  Show Sympathy

Any demonstration of sympathy towards us is regarded as weakness on our part. It also signifies that we have been successful in causing you to feel sorry for us. You may find it surprising that since we regard ourselves as superior to others that we could countenance sympathy being exhibited towards us. Surely having someone feel sorry for us amounts to an admission of weakness? You may have worked out by now and if you have not done so, then you should be aware that hypocrisy is not something that troubles our consciences. This state of affairs is because we do not possess a conscience. However, in this instance this is not hypocrisy because we are not seeking sympathy because we are actually upset. We are not sad nor are we distraught. Instead we are manufacturing a state of affairs purely in order to manipulate you into giving us what we want.

Showing sympathy towards us is providing us with attention and consequently that is entirely acceptable. We will occasionally play the victim card. You may be surprised that we do not play it as often as we do. We regard the world as against us. We are at war with the world because it is a harsh, inhospitable place that has only ever shown us disdain and cruelty. It has not shown that it cares one iota for us and therefore in order to survive we have to rely on our own resources and innate superiority to rise above the savage treatment it has meted out towards us. Nobody cares for us; so why should we accord such behaviour towards anyone else? They do not deserve a caring attitude from us, of course that presupposes that we actually know how to care about anybody other than ourselves.

We remember each and every sleight, all the injustice and unfair behaviours that have been directed at us. We are victims of the dismissive and haughty attitudes of others and rightly feel aggrieved. We do not however like to show this, because to do so is to exhibit weakness and we are not weak. No, we are far from weak. Instead, we use our status as the ultimate victims selectively. We will draw on that sense of injustice when it suits us and that is often when we find ourselves in a position of last resort.

If our vast array of manipulative techniques has been deployed but they have failed, for whatever reason, to provide us with the response that we demand and require, then we are placed in a position of last resort. We have failed to persuade, cajole, bully or intimidate to secure our aims. This means we must play our victim card and seek to evoke sympathy from you. We know that people cry when they are upset and we have seen how people react to those who are upset. They invariably offer sympathy and try and find a way of alleviating their sadness

. I watched my sister do this when she was a child. If she was upset, she would always run to my father, not our mother and he would distract her, provide her with a treat or allow her to do the thing she had been forbidden from doing in order to stop her crying. I once asked her why she cried. She explained that it was because she was sad and frightened. I asked her to expand on what she meant by sad and she said that this was when she felt lonely and that nothing was going her way. I understood what she meant by that but I never felt compelled to cry. I realised however that turning on the waterworks was an effective learned behaviour to get people to do what I wanted. I kept that lesson in my array of talents. Whilst I poured scorn on others for crying (although I delighted in seeing people do it when I was the source of their upset) I knew that it was the best way of generating sympathy when all else seemed lost.

Accordingly, whenever I felt myself in a position whereby I was going to lose out and one where I could not use some other form of manipulation to secure my aims, I would recall that sensation of all the injustices I had experienced and the tears would flow. Admittedly, there were times where I wanted to laugh because the effect was so effective and I had to turn away for fear that my ruse would come undone by my amusement. Each time I would commence my crying the sympathy would flow and I would eventually get my way. You would back down on the stance that you were adopting. You would decide against leaving me. You would give me another chance. I equate sympathy to getting my own way and I know the easiest way to generate sympathy; cry.

As an empath, you find it impossible to resist my tears and upset. With your overwhelming urge to heal and help, you want the tears to stop and you want people to be happy. You will wrack your brains to find a way to achieve that and you will bend over backwards in order to alleviate the upset. That means you have given in to me, my manipulation has worked and this asserts my superiority once again.

I will garner sympathy any way I can. I will triangulate and complain to others about your behaviour to me and make repeated mention of everything that I have done for you. I will remind you of all the support and generosity I have shown towards you (which of course was purely for the purposes of seducing you whilst conveniently ignoring the horrible treatment that I have meted out towards you). I will embark on a smear campaign explaining how hard done to I have been. I look for sympathy from any quarter as this attention provides me with fuel. The most potent sympathy however must come from you. If you show me sympathy you are confirming to me that my manipulation of you has been successful, you are giving in to what I want and you are also providing me with attention.

By being sympathetic towards us you are also reminding us of the reason why we despise you. You are weak and pathetic and we hate you for it. Yes, we want your sympathy because it works for us to enable us to get what we want but by the same token, by acting in a sympathetic fashion you are underlining the reason why we want to crush you. You will no doubt regard this as an illogical stance, but it is not in our world. It is entirely appropriate because it provides us with what we want whilst supporting out view of you and thus our superiority over you.

You will have noticed how we are never sympathetic. We do not know how to show such an emotion. In part, we are frustrated that you are able to behave in this manner and we cannot. Yes, we do not want to show sympathy but that is not the point. You are able to do something we cannot do and we do not like it. Even though it is something we do not want to do, it undermines, in our mind, our superiority to you. It is similar to us being full but still eating the extra steak to show that we can and you cannot have it. We are not enjoying that steak and we do not need it, but we will still take this step in order to assert our superiority to you.

When you show us sympathy, although we may want it, you are showing us something we cannot do and that in turns annoys us and will make us subsequently lash out at you even when you are showing us a caring and tending nature. That is how perverse our behaviour is. We know you regard it as such as you tell us this. We disagree. We think it is entirely an appropriate way to respond. Remember, we are always right.

The provision of sympathy by us is a superfluous state of affairs. It serves no purpose to us and therefore we see no reason to engage in it. If it is not generating fuel for us, then we will not do it. We are not going to engage in behaviour, which is a sign of weakness either. That would make us as weak as you and we will not allow that to happen, because it cannot happen. We are cut from a far superior cloth to you and we must repeatedly remind you of that fact.

Causing you to give me sympathy means that I have conned you once again. We know how hard it is for you to resist treating someone kindly when they exhibit distress. With us, however, it is not real distress. It is entirely manufactured. Like much of what we are, it is a fabrication that has been brought about to further out own twisted aims. We do not know what genuine sadness is. Yes, we may feel hard done to, we will experience frustration and a sense of unfairness but true sadness is an alien concept to us. Our tears are very much from the crocodile and by showing us sympathy you have allowed us to succeed again.

## 12 Neglect Your Needs

One of the effects of our behaviour is that we cause you to look at everything through our eyes. We want this to happen so that you adopt a way of living that is closest to what we need to provide us with our precious fuel. We want you to anticipate what we want. We want you considering the best way of accommodating us. To achieve this, we deploy our various methods of manipulation to make you put us at the forefront of your mind. Each day you will be thinking how best you can please us. You will be considering what must be done to avoid enraging us. You need to ascertain the steps you can take to prevent us from casting you to one side, like a spent cartridge. These mean that you put us before you. You scurry around attending to our needs, catering for our whims and second-guessing everything that we do. Not only are you displacing your needs by undertaking this approach, it is so exhausting in nature that you are left with little or no time to attend to yourself. This leads to a state of affairs where you neglect your needs.

As I have mentioned, as an empathic individual, you do enjoy putting others before yourself. That is something that is ingrained in your nature. You are able to do this, in a healthy setting, without harming or neglecting yourself. When you become involved with my kind and me, your desire to put us before yourself has a terrible consequence. We keep on taking and taking but we do not give back.

How does this neglect manifest? Initially, it will be in the form of you reducing and then extinguishing your interests and life outside of you and me. You will spend less time with your family and friends. You stop attending the amateur dramatics club that you once enjoyed. You decide against attending the theatre or a sporting event as you once normally did. Your attendance at the gym or evening class becomes intermittent before petering out altogether. You do not mind as you tell yourself that you are changing the interest.

Whereas once you engaged in pottery classes to fill an otherwise unoccupied Wednesday evening, you now have me to spend time with instead. It is a swap. As ever, my salami-slicing tactic impinges on you. First the friendships and external interests are eradicated. Next you cease to read the books you enjoy at home as I always find some task or chore for you to undertake. I may insist that you sit and watch a particular film or television programme with me even though I know you do not like it. Once upon a time you might have sat and read your book or gone into a different room and surfed the Internet. I have cut those interests of yours away through the application of my manipulative ways.

I suggest to you what you should wear for work and fly into a rage if you try to resist my control of you. You have no interest in a battle each time you want to wear a particular outfit so you accede to my demands. Knowing that I now have you bound to me, with next to nothing amounting to an interest or a form of stimulation away from me, I am able to pursue my campaign of eradication further.

I increase my demands on you. I want the house looking immaculate all the time. I call from my work place and insist on elaborate dinners that I know will take you a long time to prepare. I suggest DIY tasks that you should undertake on the basis that the money we saved could be spent on something to treat us later in the year. Of course this will not manifest. My aim is to occupy you. You become so busy looking out for me, from the moment that you wake, you barely have time to wash and eat in the morning.

Your heightened state of anxiety leads to you having a diminished appetite. That is just as well. I have been repeatedly criticising your appearance, suggesting to you that you have gained weight and passing compliments about ridiculously slender colleagues (who are incidentally fictitious) and fearful of further criticism or even of losing me, you have been eating less as a consequence. This leaves you feeling exhausted but the list of chores seems endless and the time in which you have to do them, coupled with my insistence that you work, results in you becoming zombie-like in appearance. You rarely apply any make up anymore and you select clothing, which is quick to put on for around the house and dowdy clothing for work at my prescription. Your hair has not seen a stylist in months. The once glossy, well-maintained mane is instead scrunched up on your head, straw-like and untidy.

The bags around your eyes are testament to your exhaustion and the pallid complexion you exhibit demonstrates your failure to eat properly. You will not notice this gradual decline because it is achieved over time and is subtle. Little by little you lose a part of yourself. Your interests wither away, your independence evaporates, your self-esteem lies battered and you find even the most basic of needs (shelter, warmth and food) are being rationed or denied by my treatment of you. On numerous occasions I have kicked you out of the house and you have slept in the car, fearful of approaching those now estranged friends and family members.

It is only the chance meeting with a friend when I have set you on an errand that they express shock at your appearance. You mutter excuses, brainwashed by my behaviour, unable to think straight through the fog of confusion I have developed you in. The dull ache in your forehead, which has been there for weeks (as a result of exhaustion and under eating) means you cannot muster the energy or coherence to fight back. The friend tries to intervene but I am able to persuade you, since you are in such a weakened state, that they are to be ignored and I am able to keep them at arms' length through a dose of nastiness towards them.

You become a shell. You are an automaton that has been programmed just to do what I want. Speak when spoken to, take the savage words when I dole them out, mumble an apology and try harder. Think this sounds extreme? It is not. This is what will happen if you do not ensure that your needs are attended to from the off. Be aware that we want you to neglect your needs. The less time you have for yourself means the more you have for us. The less time you have for yourself, the weaker and more run down you will become and thus you become more compliant for our requirements. It will happen. It is subtle and insidious but ever so dangerous. Look after yourself because we will not.

## 13 Challenge Us

There are two distinct reasons why you should not challenge us. The first, akin to trying to reason with us, is that it is futile. The second reason is that when you challenge us you fall into our trap of providing us with fuel.

When you try and reason with us that is an act that is taken by you in a reasonable, generally neutral manner. You advance a point in a calm and measured fashion (at least at first until we start to manipulate your emotional responses) and try to have us understand the logic of the situation in the hope that we will agree with the stance you have adopted. It is low down on the scale of argumentative behaviour. You have seen above how we respond to this reasonable manner of yours. Accordingly, should you challenge us our response is hardly going to improve is it?

Once again, our innate sense of superiority means that we do not regard ourselves as susceptible to challenge. We are unimpeachable. Nobody is allowed to question our conduct or behaviour, least of all you. We are better than you and therefore your default setting is that you are wrong and we are right. Should you attempt to challenge what we have said or done, this offends our noble standing. The challenge does not necessarily need to be directed at us. Even if it is indirect we will view it as a threat to our position. For instance, if you asked,

"Not many of your friends attended the party last night, why do you think that was?"

We will see that as you challenging the strength of our friendships. Your question is directed at the behaviour of our friends, not us, but we will still regard it as you issuing a challenge to our ability to command friends, our charisma and our appeal. In many instances, the level of offence is such that we will not even bother to deny what you are challenging us about. In one situation you may comment,

"You came in rather late last night, where did you get to?"

You may have intended this sentence as a fair comment. We did arrive late last night it was nearly 1am. The question may also be framed politely as you have asked where we went. You may be interested in what was entertaining us until that time, was it a particularly good bar or club? We do not like to be questioned. In our minds, your comment was,

"What the hell do you think you were doing coming in at that ungodly hour? That is a ridiculous time? I suppose you were out drinking and whoring as usual weren't you?"

We miss entirely the content of what you have asked. All we hear is a challenge and thus we react with offence. Our rising anger means that we are not interested in issuing a denial (futile as it maybe although that never concerns us) and instead we will immediately move to project onto you and shift the blame.

"I seem to remember you crawling in after 2am a few weeks ago (it was actually a year last month) and throwing up everywhere (you didn't). Who do you think you are to question me about where I have been?"

We deliberately go on the attack. We do not regard you as having any legitimate standing by which you can challenge us. We also know that you being the type of person that you are you will react in a certain way. Rather than brushing our remark aside and pointing out that your question was just asking what we had been doing without any insinuation of wrongdoing or blame you will defend yourself.

"What are you talking about? I haven't been out in months and I wasn't throwing up. Mind you, I seem to recall you doing that last week or have you conveniently forgotten about that?"

Another challenge is issued. The point about our late arrival the previous night has been forgotten about. Logic and reason has been dispensed with. Instead, the discussion has been plunged firmly into the arena of emotion. Exactly what we like. Accordingly, it is futile to challenge us since we will not allow you to debate the real issue. Instead we will deflect from you questioning us, by going on the attack and the point of the discussion becomes lost.

Once again we will demonstrate the infuriating duality that is a cornerstone of our behaviour. On the one hand we reject you have the basis for challenging us but at the same time we want you to do so because it enables us to go on the attack, blame you and deflect the real reason for the discussion or argument. Furthermore, it enables us to garner delicious fuel. We attack you and you feel that you have to defend yourself. You become frustrated by our comments and accusations. You are hurt, angry and upset. All of this is precisely what we want and what we aim to engineer in such a situation. By entering into challenging and questioning us, you have enabled us to move the conversation into emotional territory. We want to see your face scrunched up in rage, we desire those tears to trickle down your cheeks and for you to shout and wave your arms about. We have caused this. See how powerful and mighty we are? This makes us feel fantastic, empowered and supplied with fuel. We will aim to perpetuate the argument, goading you into keep challenging us. Each time we are mortally offended that we do so and thus in our minds our response is entirely appropriate. How dare you question us? You have now brought our barbed attack on yourself and happily this makes you react in an emotional sense and you give us fuel. You keep trying to win the argument, but as I have pointed out above, this is impossible. You are wasting your time but we want you to keep trying. We may even offer you some chink of hope by saying,

"I sort of see what you mean but what about...."

We make you think you are getting somewhere but we end the sentence with another attack against you. You decide to press on thinking you have made a gain, when really you have just consented to providing us with more fuel.

You must not challenge us. You will get nowhere in doing so. All you will do is make yourself frustrated, upset and angry. We will just sit back and drink in the fuel you are giving us. We win yet again.

## 14 Try to Understand Us

This is one of the major faults you have. It is understandable that you do this. You are an empathic individual and you take pride in helping others. In order to do this, you like to understand how people behave. What makes them tick? Why do they act as they do? You firmly believe that there is a reason behind why people take certain courses of action. Whilst it is true that there are reasons behind the way we act (indeed my publications are aimed at spreading information about that) you should not waste your time in thinking that our behaviours are linked to the reason and logic that operates in your world. We do not reside there. We live in our own created fantasy world where different rules entirely apply.

I am giving you an insight through my writing as to what those different rules are but do not try and make any sense of them. You are trying to do so by looking at them from your worldview. That is not going to help. It is like trying to read a book wearing the wrong type of spectacles. You might be able to see the shapes that are the letters and the words on the page before you, but they will not make any sense to you.

The person you see most of does not really exist and therefore it is pointless trying to understand something from your point of view that does not exist. We are created from pieces of other people. We see what we like in others and appropriate that for ourselves. Our sense of business success is lifted from our CEO. Our cousin who is an outstanding sportsman provides another part. The comedic friend gives us another shard to use in our creation. On it goes as we collect piece after fragment from all of those around us.

We do not select the whole of the individual but rather we identify certain attributes we admire and decide we would like to be seen like that. A sliver from that person, a shard from her and a splinter from him. If you look at each fragment you can make sense of it. You are looking at our brilliant record of passing music exams. You can understand that, yet when you look for the segment that show us playing the piano to concert level standard it is missing. We do not possess it and this does not make sense. Surely that part of our being exists if we have passed all those exams?

When you look at us as a whole what you are seeing is not one person but rather a myriad of individuals pieced together in a haphazard and often contradictory fashion. How can that fragment detailing what a brilliant animal hunter I am sit with that other shard proclaiming my work with conservationist charities? It makes no sense. It cannot do so because all you are seeing are the reflections of many people. You are viewing other people and not me.

The position is complicated further because all of these thousands of pieces have to be held in place each and every day. That is an exhausting and ultimately impossible task. The glue that holds them together is the fuel that we obtain from our victims. The requirement is high and huge amounts of fuel are needed to maintain the artificial edifice. This is why our behaviour is so completely self-centred. A piece begins to slide and we need the fuel to anchor it back in place. We must find that fuel or risk exposing what lurks beneath. We have no time for anything else. Fuel is everything.

We make the situation complex because we do not want you to understand us. We do now want you prying beneath the mirrored tiles and analysing what is to be found there. We do not contemplate what we are either. Yes, we know something of what we are but the dread that seizes us when we inadvertently embark on a rare act of introspection is so great that we shut it down within moments. We do not want to understand ourselves and we have no desire at all to allow you to either. That is why the myriad of pieces keeps changing, that is why we put up smoke screens, and we divert and deflect, chop and change and become the ultimate chameleon. Wheels turn within wheels, sometimes clockwise, sometimes anti-clockwise and sometimes in both directions. How can that be possible? How can someone behave the way we do? It happens; you have witnessed it.

We have to be the ever-changing conundrum. We are the unsolvable puzzle. You will exhaust yourself trying to figure it out. You will eventually (often after the event, although through my writing you will learn more at an earlier stage) grasp certain behaviours but the full picture will always be obscured. The curtain may slide back slightly giving you a glimpse, a spotlight may shine on another section and provide brief illumination but everything is always changing, rotating, spinning, clouding, obscuring and altering. It is dizzying, disorientating and deliciously difficult.

From time to time the fuel is not there in the desired quantities. You may not be providing the levels we need or perhaps other sources of supply have suddenly dried up for us before we have been able to replace them. This spells disaster for us. The edifice that we have created starts to crumble and crack. This means the fragments start to fall away. They crack or drop and thus what is underneath becomes visible for the first time. The creature that lurks in the darkness is a bundle of hatred, malevolence, envy and pain. It does not want your prying eyes to look upon it and thus it will lash out at you hoping that your response generates the fuel so the fallen piece can be shoved back into place and the gap filled. You will not understand where this creature comes from. You will not comprehend what it is, why it exists and what it does. You will be focussed instead on wondering why we behaved in that way which is at such odds with the way you have been treated before.

So far all that you have seen is the brilliant us, the wonderful us and the loving us that is reflected from the mirror pieces that we have assembled. The provision of fuel is high and the fragments remain in place. You believe you are seeing us; you have not yet realised that this is just a myriad of stolen identities. When the lurking creature is exposed, you do not realise that it is the creature, you are not aware that this is the real us. You are too caught up in wondering how this contrarian has appeared and why its behaviour is at odds with everything that you have witnessed so far. Indeed, you will consider (because this is the type of person that you are) are you to blame in some way? Did you cause this to happen? Have you knocked the piece away through something you said or did? That is what will be occupying your mind and as ever you will be focussed on making matters right again.

Although you will receive repeated glimpses of the creature from beneath, you will still not be able to comprehend what it is as you remain fascinated by the mirror pieces. Those are much more pleasant and you want those, not this craven beast that keeps appearing. You will over time, by reading and listening to others, understand the behaviours that manifest. You will gain comprehension as to why we act in a certain way. There is no logic to our behaviour but you will at least know the causes, but that is the best that you can hope for.

Trying to understand what we actually are is impossible when you are with us because we are a shapeshifter. Everything is moving at once. Our myriad pieces shift and turn. They drop off and are then replaced. The creature lashes out and then disappears. It is utterly confusing and when looked at through the lens of your understanding, it makes no sense at all. Trying to grasp what we are in order to understand us when you are in our grip is a fruitless task. You will spend so much time debating our contradictions, ruminating on the wild and sudden changes that occur and most likely seeking counsel from those who have no concept of what we are either. The blind will lead the blind.

You are better served understanding how our behaviours arise, what you need to do to cope with them or escape from them and resign gaining a true understanding of what we are to the rubbish bin. You need your energy for more important things. I know this will fly in the face of your desire to understand and help but you cannot truly ever understand what we are. We do not know ourselves so how could you possibly understand?

## 15 Accept the Blame

Do not accept the blame for the way that we are or the way that we behave. It is common for you to do this. This again is a situation that we have engineered. The way in which we subject you to the golden period when we seduce you is so utterly magnificent that the fall when we commence our devaluation of you is long and hard. At the time virtually nobody subjected to this volte-face in our behaviour has any idea what is happening to him or her. It makes no sense at all. How can someone be so wonderful and loving and then change like the flicking of a switch? It is not normal. Indeed, you have hit the nail on the head. It is not normal and neither are we. Unfortunately for you, you will not have worked out that this is our standard modus operandi. Instead, you will reach the conclusion that must have done something wrong.

Once again this ability to be self-critical is something peculiar to your kind. It is yet another reason why we choose you over others. We know that rather than point the finger at us you will look to yourself and you always find something that you have done or said that you can attach blame to. As I have mentioned earlier, your view of the world is that everything has to have a reason (and a logical one at that) why it has happened or happens. You like order, you find comfort in the natural progression of things and you have to understand. Our behaviour makes no sense but you are unable to park the matter and just shrug and accept that is just the way it is. You need to find a reason for it. You will always find that the reason is you.

This state of affairs is bolstered by our repeated capacity to blame you as well. Again and again we shower comments towards you that pin the blame on you.

"If you loved me you would understand."

"Why do you make me lose my temper?"

"I do so much for you and you still annoy me. What is wrong with you?"

"Now look what you have made me do."

By maintaining this tirade of blame (in conjunction with all our other manipulative methods that are designed to wear you down and control you) you will eventually always blame yourself. It will get to the point whereby the first word out of your mouth will be sorry. Not only that, you will find yourself apologising many times a day. You will be stunned at the level to which you will descend as you are on the receiving end of the blame game. The trivial items you not only accept responsibility for but also apologise for will leave you both astounded and perturbed. Such examples of this diminution in self-esteem are: -

"Sorry your coffee was cold, I should have realised you would have been longer on the telephone and made you a fresh one."

How on earth could you ascertain how long I would be on the telephone? Of course, you have got your apology in first because you know that if you did not, then more insults and blame labelling would follow. Potentially with even worse consequences.

"Sorry I didn't wake you in time for the match, I somehow fell asleep."

You fell asleep because you were up all night caring for our baby, single handedly as usual. Of course, it is beyond my wit to set an alarm. Why would I do that when I can find another task for you to do that gives me attention and the potential to demean you if you make a mistake?

"Sorry I didn't add garlic to your meal, I forgot."

You forgot because last week I wanted garlic and the week before that I did not. The reality is that if you had added it I would have criticised you and blamed you for ruining the meal. If you forgot the garlic, I would criticise you and blame you for ruining the meal. When it has got to the stage whereby you are apologising for the most minor of transgressions (most of which are not your fault or even worthy of apportioning blame) you have no fight left in you and you just accept that it must be your fault. Combine this with the gas lighting that we will be subjecting you to and we will have you apologising for claiming black is black when we say that it is white. You may read this with astonishment if this has not happened to you, but those of you who have been entwined by my kind will know full well how it is always your fault. Each and every time. This matrix of blame is created from the following: -

1. We will always blame you irrespective of the circumstances;

2. You are naturally predisposed to being self-critical;

3.  You need to find a cause for behaviour. You cannot logically attribute it to what we do so you conclude it must be you;

4.  You are told so often that you are at fault you eventually accept this must be so; and

5.  Your coping mechanisms have been totally eroded.

None of this is your fault. You might have seen the red flags but not paid attention to them. That is not your fault, we sought to obscure them and persuade you to ignore them. You failed to listen to the warnings your family gave about me. That is not your fault. We whispered in your ear that they were jealous and causing trouble. You had a feeling something was not right but you did not pay attention to your gut instinct. That is common and unsurprising in view of our onslaught of affection when we love bomb you.

You are made to think that if you try that bit harder, consider the consequences of your conduct at every stage, second guess how we might react and look at the world through our eyes you will do enough to return to the golden period. The fact this has not happened yet must be down to you, surely? It is not the case.

We blame because we want you to feel bad. We want you try harder. We want you walking on eggshells. Your tears when you mouth another apology make us feel powerful because we have reduced you to this state. We jerk the strings and you do the dance for us and if you do not move fast enough, well that is your fault, not ours, even though we are the one controlling you. Blaming you deflects from our many faults. It keeps you subjugated and downtrodden. It reinforces our sense of superiority.

Always remind yourself that nothing you have done has been your fault. You are far too hard on yourself. It is our fault. Who hurls the insults? Who shouts? Who slaps you? It is we. Nobody deserves to be subjected to such treatment and especially not from someone who is meant to love you. The first time you apologise when you have done nothing wrong is the time we scent blood. We have landed the blow and we will do it over and over again. We know, because of the type of person that you are, that you will ultimately accept that you are at fault. It is just a question of time before we have you saying sorry. We will chip away at you repeatedly until you apologise and then we turn away from you and smile. Mission accomplished. It really is the thin end of the wedge and once you have said sorry once you will say it so many times and in so many situations.

You must never apologise to us. As with most of our behaviours, it has at least two effects. It gives us fuel and it has you subjected to our control. You have to maintain an implacable position whereby you are not to blame. No matter how much pressure we subject you to, you cannot concede. The instant you do; it is like a leak springing in a dam. The trickle becomes a stream, which becomes a torrent and then a flood. Once you give an inch we will, as the saying suggests, take a mile.

Do not blame yourselves for what we are or what we do. The fault always lies with us.

## 16 Try to Change Us

Of the myriad of things, you must not do with our kind, this perhaps ranks as one of the greatest mistakes you can make and thus one, which has to be avoided. I may as well tell you straight away. We cannot change. We do not want to change and we cannot change.

Why do we not want to change? Change requires energy and commitment. We do not like using our energy for anything other than acquiring fuel. As for commitment, we are not the type of people who understand the nature of commitment. We are always about the short-term. We want instant gratification and anything that requires a sustained effort is too great an enterprise for us and not something we will ever undertake. Our focus is the acquisition of fuel. This is such an all-consuming task we do not have any time or energy to do anything else, even if we were minded to do so. This position applies to most of our kind. There is no desire to change because it is too difficult and distracts from the quest for fuel.

We will not change because we enjoy what we are. We revel in the admiration that we obtain from everyone we meet. We are kings of our warped castle, masters of the fantasy we survey and the supreme authority. We are gods. Why would we ever want to alter that state of affairs? When you are at the top why would you want to give that up? We are the best and have no desire to change that position. You may raise the question what about the creature that lurks within, beneath the façade and underneath the mask? Would we not want to change what that is? The answer to that is no. We deny its existence. We do not want to be troubled by being reminded about this dark beast that exists. In fact, its existence is the construct of others. It is the fault of other people and the way that we have been treated that created this thing. You and others keep trying to awaken it, it is part of your conspiracy against us. It will not work and you will not succeed. We are cleverer than you. We see you and have you in our eye. You cannot outwit us by trying to make out that we are something that we are not. We know you do it deliberately to try and put us down but we are better than you. We are superior.

That creature which you have created can be kept locked away anyway. Its appearance is down to you. Provide us with fuel and it will not appear. Deny us that fuel and it tries to appear. See how it is your fault once again? We do need to change because there is nothing wrong with us. This supposed flaw is not we, it is you. We know we are the best, the champion, the master.

Turning our attention to the malign variety of our kind, not only do we enjoy what we are as I have explained above, we enjoy what we do. We absolutely relish the power we wield over you. We find pleasure in seeing you angry, upset and hurt. It causes a surge of power and strength through us. We revel in constructing the games that we subject you to. Treating people like chess pieces amuses us, all of you pawns to our solitary king. Hither and zither we move you, our puppets at our control, as we smile malevolently whilst we destroy lives. We have no desire at all to relinquish this power and satisfaction. The lesser narcissist does not want to change because it requires too much effort and is a waste of energy. The malign narcissist does not want to change because this is our calling. We enjoy our position, our power and our machinations.

Not only do we not want to change we cannot change. You must understand this. We know (and we play on this trait of yours – as we do with all of your good and positive traits) that you are a caregiver, a healer and a soother. It is central to your beliefs that people can be made better. Not only do you believe this, we have conned you into thinking that we can be changed because we once showed you a wonderful, kind, attentive and loving person. That person was not we. It was an illusion. As I have explained above, that person is the product of a thousand different attributes from many, many different people and there is nothing of us there. We chose all the good, kind and decent elements from people. We know from our keen observation of other people how to act in a loving fashion. Our dark skills are honed in order to seduce you and make you think that we are heaven sent.

One of the most difficult things for you to ever grasp is that this was not real. Surely nobody could fabricate that intensity of love and affection could they? Yes, they can and yes we did. We have duped you into thinking this person was real and you think that if this person loved you once in such a magnificent fashion they can do so again. You think we can be fixed and return to that person. This will not happen. You cannot change us into something that never existed in the first place.

Our behaviours are hard-wired into us. Not only can you not change us back to that person you thought existed; you cannot change what we are in any event. You are attempting to halt an unstoppable force. The way we are is not capable of being altered, changed or varied. Our conduct is ingrained and threaded through our DNA. There is no hope to effect a change. Few will listen to that of course, but this is your chance to pay attention. If you try to change what we are you will only be submitting yourself to a sustained period of agony, hurt and exhaustion.

You know we like to play games and we know that you are trying to make us something else. We will play along with this as part of our aim to get you to remain with us. We will say such things as,

"I want to be a better person. Please help me."

"Please will you save me; you are the only person who can."

"I will change this time. I promise."

"I know what I do, I cannot help it, but with your help I can improve."

These and the other similar statements of intent are all empty. Do not make the mistake of thinking that we really do want to change. As I have explained above, we do not want to. All we do is say these things because we know you want to hear us say it. It appeals to your good-hearted nature. You must understand that: -

1.  It is your nature that makes you want to heal us;

2.  We have conned you though the golden period into thinking that we can be changed;

3.  We do not want to be changed because it is too hard to achieve;

4.  We do not want to be changed because we enjoy what we are and what we do;

5. Even in the unlikely event we did want to change, we cannot.

Do not make the mistake and be misled by those who claim they have changed our type. They have not. What may have happened has been a natural waning of the behaviours with the advancement of age. It does not happen with all narcissists, but with some, there is a softening of behaviours, but there is never a complete eradication of the narcissistic behaviour. In others, the narcissist may just be duping them further in order to fulfil an ulterior motive. Finally, those who claim they have changed the narcissist may have actually altered their own behaviour, which has lessened the impact of the narcissist's conduct, and thus they think it is the narcissist has changed. They have not.

The only thing that you can change is you. You can change the way you behave to escape us or at the very least ameliorate the impact of our behaviour on you. Do not make the mistake of thinking that we will change. We will not and we cannot.

## 17 Pander to Us

We expect you to pander to our every whim. We are important. You are not. We see you as an appliance that churns out fuel for us and since you are nowhere near as important as we are; your role is to run around after us. Our energies have to be channelled towards gaining fuel. This means we do not have the time, energy or inclination to do much else. Accordingly, you must wait on us. Not only that, we expect you to always do what we want.

Similar to our approach with regard to you accepting the blame, once we know that you will do anything we want in order to please us, we will keep demanding that you do it over and over again. We expect you to pander to us in the following ways: -

1. Acting as our personal servant;

2. Allowing us to do what we want;

3. Placating us when we lose out tempers.

Of all our behaviours and expectations, the need for you to pander to us is the one which is most aligned to our infantile outlook. Children begin their lives exhibiting narcissistic traits because everything has to revolve around them. They must be fed, cleaned, kept warm, entertained, taught to walk and talk. It is all about them. A child is unable to survive otherwise. These shackles are eventually thrown off as the child grows and matures, a healthy outlook in life causing it to realise that one must give as well as take. We see this in others but it is not applicable to our kind. We continue to make those infantile demands. We want you to cook for us, carry out attending to our laundry, bring us drinks, clean our home, run our errands and give us the fuel.

Why do we expect you to pander to us?

1. We are special and as such should be accorded special treatment;

2. You are our appliance and there to serve us;

3. You must supply us with fuel, that is your role;

4. It is second nature to you as a care giver; and

5. Periodically we are affected by the helplessness of being an infant.

I have repeatedly mentioned that we are special and have huge sense of entitlement, so I need not mention that further.

Once again we know that your kind loves to help people. You obtain satisfaction from doing things for other people and you do not mind doing so without reward. The pleasure you obtain from such selfless acts is the reward in itself. It is natural for you to want to reach out and help somebody, to ease his or her pain and assist that person. As with everything we do with you, we take advantage of this trait.

You make the error of pandering to us as an immediate response to our temper tantrums. In the same way that a frustrated parent grows tired of the tears and screaming of a badly behaved child, you grow tired and fearful of the shouting and threats. You prefer calm and you want to ensure that everything is all right. In tandem with your self-critical behaviour, you feel that you must have done something wrong and therefore it is incumbent on you to put things right. You accordingly give in to our selfish demands in order to keep the peace. Once we know this is how you react we will keep on throwing the tantrums and expecting you to soothe us. You see that it works so you decide that it is the path of least resistance. Give us what we want and the tirade of abuse ends. Except it will not. It will rear its head again in the future because we want to flex our muscles and watch you jump at our command.

We use you to provide fuel. That is expected of you. When you pander to us you give us attention and in turn this generates the fuel.

The need for you to pander us is also necessary to address our sensation of being a child. By this I do not mean the temper tantrums that we exhibit, although they are of a childish nature. There are occasions where we feel helpless and pathetic, like a young child. It is an awful sensation and one that we hate. It reminds us of weakness, which is something that we abhor.

When it does manifest we are taken back to feeling small, lost and helpless. Not only is that sensation unpleasant in itself it also offends the fact that we are powerful and superior. Being made to feel like that is unfair and wrong. We find it repugnant. It is therefore necessary to expel that sensation as quickly as possible. The most effective way to achieve this is to obtain fuel from you, but it is extremely preferable if this fuel arises from you pandering to our needs. We feel parented, soothed and protected. Our special status is reinstated and the horrible sensation ebbs away. Some of our kind will expect their own children to parent them when this sensation arises. It does not matter where the pandering originates from, so long as someone is making us feel that we are being looked after.

By pandering to us you are also eroding your self-esteem. You are taking a backwards step each time we get you to give in. Our demands are outrageous, our accusations scandalous and our treatment of you is abhorrent. Nevertheless, you will keep doing it and little by little we chip away at your sense of self. We do this because we want to subsume you into us. We ultimately do not differentiate between what you are and what we are. We fail to recognise that you are your own person. That does not accord with what we need. You are there to provide fuel for us and you are there to do what we want.

Do not pander to us. We will expect it all the more and you will find yourself running around in circles after us as your sense of self vanishes.

## 18 Show Upset

We are predators. Predators normally seek out prey that is weaker than them in order to ensure that they succeed in catching that prey. We are different. We prefer you to be strong to begin with. This means that you have far more fuel to give, that you will try harder to please us, that you will go the extra mile to appease us and pull up trees in order to try and fix us. This strength and depth of character (not something we are blessed with) means that you are a deep and delicious reservoir of fuel. Your strength does not however translate into being able to resist us. Your fortitude does not manifest in insurmountable defences. You do not see us coming; indeed, it is very difficult to identify us amidst the love bombing, certainly without any prior knowledge of our kind. Accordingly, no matter how strong a person you are, no matter how independent of spirit you might be and someone who knows their own mind, this will not protect you when we come sniffing around you. Instead, it means we have more to draw out of you and that pleases us.

We want you to be strong because we cannot stand weakness. It reminds us too often of the thing that we fear the most. I mentioned above our hatred of that infantile moment. This is because it is weakness and we are not weak. We are superior. Anything that reminds us of weakness will cause us to react in an aggressive manner.

You will observe a strange reaction from us when you cry. For an instant we are paralysed with indecision as we are caught up in considering the appropriate response.

1. If we have not caused your upset, we know from our observation of others that the appropriate response is to comfort you, soothe you and see what can be done to alleviate the upset. If others are present, this requirement (and especially our need to maintain our respectable public face) becomes all the more pressing. We however, not dealing in any empathic response, do not instinctively react to reach out to you. We have to process it; and

2. Your tears irritate us. We hate to see the weakness. We despise it and we become angry. We want you to stop. Your tears are not giving us what we want. Instead they remind us of what we are not (empathic and a caregiver) and what we fight to overcome (weak) and we hate you for it.

Trapped between the reaction we feel and the reaction that we should be providing as an apparently caring person we are left uncertain. This state of uncertainty erodes our sense of superiority and makes us begin to feel weaker. This cannot be allowed to happen. We will stand watching, an impassive expression on our face, bemused onlookers waiting for our response as we shift through this conflict inside ourselves.

Inside us the rage is coming. It is necessary to obliterate this feeling of weakness that you are forcing us to experience and we hate you for it. If time allows, we will move you somewhere private so that the forthcoming fury is not witnessed by others and our carefully constructed public façade is not damaged by the anger that will be unleashed against you. In certain cases, the incandescent rage cannot be held in check and a public dressing down ensues. We become even angrier because you have caused us to behave that way in front of others. It is your fault. You made us angry at your weakness. You caused our public image to be tarnished and we hate you all the more, unbridled fury will be the likely consequence as we seek to scorch away the feeling of weakness you have imbued in us.

The situation is different if we are alone and we have caused you to cry through our treatment of you or our particular behaviour that has hurt you. By being upset you are reinforcing your weakness. Yet again, we operate a dual policy. We want you to cry because it shows we have caused a reaction in you. It underlines how powerful we are. We know we have got to you. Conversely the fact you are crying reminds us how weak you are and in turn we become angry that we are with somebody who is this weak. It acts as a painful reminder that the lurking weakness we despise may just loom at any moment. We crave your upset to give us fuel yet at the same time we despise it since it reminds us of weakness.

We know from our observations of people that ordinarily those who are upset are to be afforded comfort and sympathy. As I have written above, that is why we produce our own crocodile tears to ensure that we are given sympathy. Do not expect that we will provide it to you. Not only do we not know the feeling of wanting to comfort somebody who is upset, our reaction is overloaded by the simultaneous sensations of power (we made you upset) and anger (your weakness offends us). You will look to us for support. You will not find it. Once again we are too busy catering to our own needs to even begin to consider yours. As our power increases from the fuel you are providing so does our irritation and then anger at how pathetic you are. This will make us lash out at you, often verbally and sometimes physically. We are caught in a dichotomy. We need your upset to give us the power but in turn it reminds us of something we do not want to countenance and therefore we unleash rage in order to try and obliterate this feeling of weakness and vulnerability that your upset state embodies. So far as you are concerned you will end up being on the receiving end of our wrath.

Do not be upset when you are with us. We will not comfort or support you. All we will do is cause you more pain and hurt you with our vicious tongue and flailing fists.

## 19 Show Intimacy

Do not show intimacy towards us. Our response will only wound you and do so severely. We do not do intimacy. Yes, we show it during our seduction of you. The heightened level of fuel we obtain from you during this initial stage overrides our general distaste for intimacy. We will touch you, kiss you, hold you and regularly make love to you. All of this is part of our ruse. By doing these things you will respond by providing us with affection, admiration and fuel. You will bond to us more quickly and more deeply, consequently becoming ensnared in our web. Once that has been achieved we will not continue with this affection and intimacy. We do not like to do it and now there is no longer any need to do so. We have achieved our aim.

Why do we dislike intimacy? It is a positive emotion and we are not wired to experience those. As with so much of our behaviour, we know, through observation and repetition, that by engaging in intimate behaviour with you, you will respond in the way we want you to. We do not feel what you tell us you feel when you are intimate with us. You explain that you feel loved, wanted, safe and happy. We do not experience any of this. To us intimacy is a vile thing. What we want is what actually flows from you when there is intimacy. That is what we are after. We feel your admiration, which fuels us and makes us feel powerful.

Not only do we not feel what you feel when there is intimacy, we experience negative feelings which cause us to be repulsed by lying close to someone, holding hands or engaging in a sensual embrace. We feel envy and irritation. This arises because you talk freely about how wonderful you feel, using the various adjectives to convey your sense of elation as we hold one another in bed on a rainy Sunday morning. We do not feel that and since we are unable to feel something that you do it suggests to us that there is something missing from us. We are incomplete. This then grows into wondering if this means that you are better in some way that we are. We equate having something to being better than somebody else. If you have emotions that we do not, then this is suggesting to us that you may be better than us in some way and we cannot countenance that. It is contrary to our innate superiority. Accordingly, we despise demonstrations of intimacy.

Once we are of the view that we no longer have to engage in this awful activity because we have achieved our aim, we will immediately halt being intimate. This has a dual benefit to us. Firstly, we do not have to undertake doing something that makes our skin crawl. Secondly, the act of withdrawal causes consternation and concern on your part. You become upset; you keep asking what is wrong and why we do not cuddle you anymore. You query why we never greet you with anything more than perfunctory kiss on the cheek. Your reaction to the cessation of this intimacy provides us with an alternative source of fuel. Thus we are doubly delighted.

Our withdrawal does mean that you crave the intimacy all the more. It was so delicious, intense and wonderful during our seduction of you;

94

you want to recover it again, as you always want to recover anything to do with the golden period. We understand that as normal individual, you want to be held, caressed and kissed. That is something most people want. We gave it to you in spades and took it to another level. You want that back. In order to try and recover the position you invariably decide that if you show us more affection and intimacy then this will trigger a return to what we used to do. Wrong. We do not want your affection any more.

We have captured you. Instead we want your emotional reaction and we get that from frustrating and upsetting you by reason of our withdrawal. When you keep appearing and hugging us from behind or lean down to kiss us as we are sat at the table you are doing one of the things we hate. There is no seduction phase fuel overload to mask the horror of it to us anymore. We do not feel what you feel, we have no need to act it out anymore and all you are doing is reinforcing that feeling we do not have. You are reminding us of the paucity of our positive emotions. In turn, you are insinuating that you are better than us. This will irritate us and then infuriate us.

Unfortunately for you, you cannot comprehend this reaction. Why would someone not want to be hugged and kissed? Who would not want to make love (and so brilliantly as we once did)? It does not equate in your normal and healthy world. Puzzled by our illogical response you decide that the answer must be to persevere. You keep on nuzzling your mouths against our necks; you try to take our hands when out walking and each night you reach out to us in the hope of initiating love making. You believe that you can rekindle that intimacy by replicating it and showing us the way. You are utterly wrong. All you are doing through this behaviour is dangling a red rag in front of us. We see you as mocking us. You keep showing off the very thing that we dislike. You keep telling us how

"I loved the way you used to me hold me tight at night, I felt so safe."

"The way you used to kiss me made me feel so special, like I was the only lady in the world for you."

"When your hand took mine I knew that everything was going to be alright. I had you to shield and protect me."

You keep saying these things alongside pushing intimacy towards us. We do not feel what you are describing and by keep doing it and telling us how you feel when it did happen you are repeatedly reminding us of a deficiency. We hate you for it.

We want to hurt you. You are hurting us and thus we want to lash out. Of course, by shrugging your arm away from us, by pushing you back or making a scathing remark you are left puzzled. Why do we keep doing this when you are being so pleasant and affectionate? You become upset and that makes us feel powerful. We lash out some more to punish you for making us feel uncomfortable, for flaunting your positive emotions in front of us and to make you more upset.

By trying to cure us with kindness all you are doing is reminding us of the things we are not and this means there can be only one response from us, to lash out at you. This makes the hurt even worse because we do it at a time when your defences are completely down, when you are being romantic and loving. Do not show any intimacy to us as you will only be hurt and come to regret it.

# 20 Compromise Your Boundaries

We do not recognise boundaries. Everything is up for grabs in our minds owing to our massive sense of entitlement. We go where we want, see whom we want and do what we want. You are in no position to challenge us, as we are superior to you. Boundary violation is second nature to us. Be it kissing a complete stranger full on the lips when we have only just met them, to attending a party we have not been invited to (and in some instances actually told we are not wanted) through to taking objects, which do not belong to us.

We are the ultimate invading army. It is important for you not to compromise your boundaries with us as (and this is so often the case with much of our behaviour) once we have violated them once, we will continue to do so and the incursions will become deeper and further. You have no prospect of recovering them. This is no battle, which will ebb and flow. No, we advance and chip away at your boundaries in furtherance of our own agendas. You need to maintain a line from the beginning and stick to that boundary.

This is difficult for you to do. We do not immediately park our tanks on your lawn so that you have to react in the strongest method available to you. We are nowhere near as obvious as that. This is a further occasion when our well-honed salami slicing tactics are deployed. There is an excellent radio and television series in the United Kingdom. It began as *Yes, Minister* and became *Yes, Prime Minister*. For those of you unfamiliar with it, it revolved around a government minister, Jim Hacker and his daily skirmishes with a senior civil servant, Sir Humphrey Appleby. Nigel Hawthorne and Paul Eddington played the parts brilliantly. Hacker would devise some new scheme or initiative (invariably geared around winning votes) and Sir Humphrey would do his level best to delay, Frustrate, obfuscate, slow down and ultimately stop the scheme.

It was a fascinating portrayal of British politics and the civil service machine. In one particular episode, Hacker is discussing the Trident nuclear deterrent with an eminent professor. The professor is trying to get Hacker to get rid of Trident because it is massively expensive and he argues that it will never be used. Nobody wants to unleash nuclear weapons. Hacker does not accept this explaining that there may come a time when he has to press the button and bring about nuclear Armageddon. The professor, in an excellent demonstration of salami slicing tactics discusses when Hacker would actually press the button.

The scenario revolves around when the Cold War between East and West was flourishing and Germany was a divided country. Berlin although in East Germany, was split between West Berlin (the democratic and capitalist side) and East Berlin (governed by dictatorship and communism). The exchange between Hacker and the professor went something like this. The Professor poses the hypothesis.

"Let us suppose there is a large fire in West Berlin, the fire brigade is struggling to contain it and therefore the East Berlin fire brigade offers assistance. Would you press the button?"

"Of course not," Hacker responds, "that would be ridiculous."

"The East German fire brigade crosses over to West Berlin to help out; do you press the button now?"

"No, don't be ridiculous."

"The East German police come across too to assist. Do you press the button?"

"No."

"The East German police start putting up some road blocks around the area affected by the fire and restrict movement through this area. Do you press the button?"

"No. Of course not."

"The East German police organise for East German troops to cross into West Berlin to assist their crowd control and policing of the area, do you press the button?"

"No."

The exchange continues in a similar vein with the Professor making a slight incursion each time and each time Hacker resolutely refuses to press the button. He does not regard the step taken, in itself, as sufficiently serious to warrant unleashing such a dramatic response. The conversation goes on until communist troops are marching through London, with Western Europe occupied and still the button has not been pressed. The professor thus concludes there is little point in having Trident, as it will never be used.

This anecdote reinforces exactly what we do. Like cutting fine slices of salami we will cut away at your boundaries pushing forward little by little on each occasion. You will not see the solitary act as one, which merits you resisting or applying your own "nuclear option", and instead you accept the incursion, then another and another.

With us it will manifest at first by using your items. We will take the last bottle of water from the fridge and not replace it. We use up your cotton buds. We move on to using your car and using up your petrol without filling it up again. Then we always insist on watching what we want on the television. After that, we want complete silence whilst we are watching our programmes. We demand to know where you are going, we disturb you at work with a minor query when you made it clear to us that morning you should not be interrupted as you had an important meeting to attend to. We go through your handbag or pockets to see what we can find. We answer for you in a group situation when somebody invites your opinion on a matter. We decide what you will have to eat when we order a take-away or at a restaurant. We deem that you have had enough to drink.

We dissuade you from having friends come round because "we want to watch the big ball game" and you compromise on this occasion, thinking that there is no harm in doing so. The problem is that it is not just this occasion. Each time we press forward and you are left having to back down, compromise and retreat as boundary after boundary is stripped away. We are entitled to do all of this and we know you will not protest because you fail to see the larger picture and you do not want to cause an unnecessary fuss since the matter in question where we are removing the boundary is not such a big deal, is it? The subtlety by which we do this means that you fail to see what is happening to you until it is far too late. How many times does that happen with the way we behave?

We stop you going out, we pick up your phone and start looking through it, and we demand your passwords so we can see what you have been doing on social media. Bit by bit we will breach your boundaries and invade every aspect of your life. We want complete hegemonic control over you. We do this as we do not recognise you as a separate person and we love to be in control. This means we are powerful and reinforces our superiority over you. There is nothing we cannot do when it comes to you.

The violations become more extreme. We do not recognise when our insulting behaviour crosses the line. We are physically violent towards you. We demand sex despite your protestations of tiredness or a lack of interest. Your interests, your possessions, your friendships, your family, your mind and your body have no fences around them as we tear them down. You have no sanctuary and nowhere sacred to hide from the storm that is us.

Never compromise your boundaries with us. Even if the incursion seems minor, always remember it is the first slice of the stick of salami and we will slice the whole thing. Resist that first cut, every time.

## 21 Expect Support

We don't provide support. We are too concerned with ourselves and our daily hunt for the fuel that we need to be concerned about you. We are engrossed in our own world and have no interest in yours. The only time we pay attention to you is when you are providing us with fuel or you stop providing us with fuel. Everything we do is focussed around us. This is because we have to obtain fuel, as without we will disintegrate. The hunger for this fuel is never ending and accordingly all of our energy must be applied towards obtaining it. This leaves us with nothing left over for anyone else.

Being a caregiver yourself, you would like to think that the person who you share your life with, or who you work closely with, would be amenable to providing you with support. That may mean giving you emotional support when you are experiencing a difficult time or taking the strain allowing you to lessen the burden on yourself. You give and you are happy to do so, therefore why should they not do so as well? That is the outlook of someone normal operating by the norms and rules of your world. Those do not apply to us. We cannot provide you with support since we have nothing available to do so.

Added to that we do not know how to provide emotional support. Yes, we can see how chores can be done and the like. We also have observed the ways that you provide emotional support to other people and we know the phrases that are used, the expressions that are formed on people's faces and the gestures that are made. We have seen all that and we could trot all that out. In fact, we have done in the past. We did this when we were seducing you. When we wanted you to divulge about your weaknesses and vulnerabilities this will have invariably saddened you and upset you. It may even have caused an episode where you need emotional support. We were happy to go through the motions then because we were at the stage of investing in you in order to get our fuel. We were content to make the right noises, give you a hug and make the panacea that is the cup of tea. All of this was learned from others. We did not feel anything for you. We could not put ourselves in your shoes (heaven forbid that would ever happen) and we could not empathise with what you were experiencing and nor can we ever do that. Yet again, we conned you into thinking that we are a caring and selfless person. We demonstrated such an approach when we were first together and that attracted you to us. This raised expectation that you could rely on us and turn to us when the need arose. It is all false.

Furthermore, when you need support and expect it from us, you are showing to us how you are weak. We despise weakness. You will find that our kind is rarely found near children, the infirm and ill and the elderly. This is because they are all weak and want support regularly. We do not want to be reminded of that fact. We cannot be bothered with you cluttering up our route to fuel. An exhibition of weakness infuriates us. A normal person would see someone in a position of weakness and deign to help and assist. We have seen how this is a natural reaction in normal people. It will not happen with us.

If you are fortunate, we will absent ourselves from the situation in an instant. We will generate some urgent reason; find a pressing engagement we had forgotten about in order to ensure we can get away from you and your ailment, woe or injury. You probably will never see us move as quick when it comes to getting away from somebody who needs help. If we are unable to exit the situation, then we may just stand and look at you. You could be reaching out to us, eyes filled with tears of pain, asking for help and we will just give you a blank stare. We know we ought to be helping you, convention and observation has told us this, but we cannot do so. We are unable to leave but we are also unable to help you. This requires compassion and we do not have any. It requires us to us our energies to help you out and we are forbidden from doing so.

Our ultimate reaction where you need support from us is to go on the offensive. The uncomfortable feeling that you have generated inside of us makes us feel less powerful and smacks of inferiority. We know of only one way to banish such a sensation. We need to reassert our power and that means we must lash out at you. It becomes necessary to subject you to further insults and denigrating comments, at a time when you are feeling hurt and vulnerable.

"What are you crying for? I have had worse happen to me."

"I am sick and tired of you being pathetic. Deal with it."

"I bet (insert name of triangulated individual) would not make such a song and dance about it like you do."

"It's only a dog, you can get another one. Seriously, what a display over a dumb animal."

"You are hysterical; you need to get help."

"Stop crying or I will give you something to cry about."

"That's right; make it about you on my special day."

We will lash out at you with these words in order to make you feel worse and ourselves feel better because that is all we care about. We fooled you into thinking that we care about you. That is a fallacy. Do not expect us to support you.

Demonstrating our legendary hypocrisy, we will expect you to always be there for us. When we have a need you must attend to it straight away, even if you are experiencing difficulties yourself. When we have a scratch we expect you to make it better even though you might be bleeding to death before us. As with so much of our behaviour we do not regard the way we act towards you as meaning you should behave the same way towards us. If you chopped us in half, you would most likely find this stencilled through us like lettering on a stick of rock

"Do as I say, not do as I do."

## 22 Don't Believe Our Insults

I have explained that above that you should not believe what we say in the context of our seduction of you. Similarly, you should not believe what we say to you when we move on to devalue you. In order to alter the method of the fuel we obtain from you, our once considerate and caring behaviour must give way to nastiness, inattention and insults.

We are experts at hurling out abuse. We prefer to cause the damage with our tongues because that uses up less energy. Some of the low functioning of our kind has a tendency to rely on their fists, I do not. I much prefer the invisible injury that a choice insult leaves on my victims. We are brilliant at issuing scathing insults because we have ascertained your weaknesses and vulnerabilities. We know which buttons to press to get the best reaction from you and accordingly extract the most potent fuel. We are fully conversant with your insecurities and your weak spots and we will exploit that knowledge to the full when we insult you.

Whether it is a back-handed compliment delivered with a smile, a sarcastic put down a full blown rant resplendent with expletives we use the delivery of insults as one of our key tools in our box of darkness. Nobody likes being insulted, but imagine what it is like when we have peered into your heart and know precisely what will have you sobbing, shouting or quaking with fear? Our insults are powerful.

We create, through the application of our manipulative methodology a false world, which we drag you into. This alien environment is one where the normal rules does not apply and you find yourself accepting what we say when we insult you as true. We browbeat you to such a degree that your self-esteem is shredded. This leaves you with no coping mechanisms that you can turn to in order to deflect our nastiness.

You might ordinarily turn to one of your friends and ask whether they think you are selfish in the way you behave, because we spent the entire previous evening telling you that you were self-centred because you wanted to watch a particular programme. We dredged up as many instances as we could muster of this fictitious selfish behaviour and directed them at you in a savage manner, coupled with unpleasant remarks about your character and looks. Once upon a time you would have brushed such comments aside in an instant. You know who you are and you know that you are a selfless, giving person. You could list a host of things that you do that reinforces your sharing nature but you do not even have to go there. You already know that you are not selfish. Whoever that person was, they no longer exist. We have you doubting who you are. You turn to a third party to obtain some validation and reassurance but this will not be forthcoming Most likely we have isolated you from these people so you have nobody to obtain the relatively impartial advice and response from. In a nightmare scenario you end up consulting with one of the many Lieutenants that we have placed so they reinforce our opinion and disagree with you.

Our repeated bombardment of you is designed to have you believing what we say is correct. Our insulting comments to you and about you take on the mantle of truth. Through our smear campaigns we tell others about how terrible you behave towards us, the inconsiderate action you engage in and the lack of appreciation for what we have done for you. Worn down through all our other actions it becomes easier to accept what we are saying about you and telling you. You have heard it so many times it must be correct, mustn't it? Not only will this continue to diminish your self-esteem it will pollute other areas of your thinking. Your thoughts are deemed to be wrong. You are mistaken in your recall and incorrect when you try to put us straight. The self-righteousness we muster when we tell you that you have misremembered something but we have come to expect that of you as you tell a lot of lies are difficult to counter. When we speak we do so as if we are the supreme authority because we regard ourselves as the supreme authority. Our word is law. You must heed it and obey it. Everything we say is a fact. Our unwavering belief in this is breath taking to behold and it will cause you, no matter how sure you might be about something, to question yourself. Perhaps we are right and you have forgotten what was said? Maybe you have heard it incorrectly?

This state of doubt and confusion stems from how we insult and demean you. You may not think it now but if you are subjected to this on a daily basis you will begin to believe the source of our viciousness towards you must be correct. If we are right about that then we must be right about other things also. This form of bullying you is insidious. It is predicated on our total conviction that we are right and we are superb at maintaining that veneer of accuracy. No wonder so many our kind become politicians. We subscribe to the view that if we tell a big enough lie about you, not only will you believe it but so will everybody else. I seem to remember an historical figure saying something similar. I wonder if he was one of us?

Do not accept what we are saying when we are raining the insults down on you as being the truth of the matter. We adopt the stance that we are always right in order to bring you under and keep you under out control. You must not accept that state of affairs.

## 23 Expect to Enjoy Birthdays

They happen every year and you have come to dread the appearance of both your own birthdays and mine. You would much rather neither take place if you are entirely honest. The day is spent treading on eggshells as you await the inevitable argument and dressing down that you will receive. The annual sense of disappointment will happen again and again and you hope somehow it will change, but it never does.

Let's begin with my birthday. You dedicate time and money to making my birthday an enjoyable and memorable occasion. I dedicate a degree of energy to ensure that it is memorable, but for the wrong reasons. You plan something special to mark the occasion and go to considerable lengths to organise a surprise party or a trip out somewhere you believe I will like. You scour catalogues and the Internet trying to find that gift you hope will make me break out in a smile. Most normal people will be happy with half the effort you put into pleasing me on my birthday. Not me. The occasion may involve a grand day out and a spectacular gift but just as it did last year and the year before that, it will end in an argument and us lashing out at you.

On the face of it, one would imagine that just for once we would get throughout the day without causing some kind of drama. After all, the day is all about us. Exactly what we like and what we want. People wish us happy birthday, they send us cards, they give us presents and you run around lifting and carrying for us (even more than usual). The spotlight is firmly on us. We drink up all this fuel but still we want more. Every single second has to be about us. Do not expect us to thank you or anyone else who provides us with a gift. Remember, we are entitled to receive them. We may have received gifts off twenty people but you know that all we will harp on about is the person we did not get a gift from whom we expected to. That becomes the focus of our irritation. The brilliant and thoughtful gifts are left to one side as we rail against this one person who has not bought us something. It does not matter that they send a card, it does not matter that we did not send them a gift on their birthday (and never have done), and it does not matter that nobody else would expect this distant relative to send such a gift. We will raise it and repeat it and rant about it.

Woe betides you if you do not give to us the exact gift we expected. If you fail to do this, we will comment and lash out at you. You cannot possibly love us since you did not give us the right gift. We conveniently ignore the fact that what you have brought us is still a wonderful gift and we actually do like it. That is not the point. It is not the gift we wanted and you will be subjected to our scathing remarks. If by sheer dint of exhaustive effort, you manage, against all the odds, to work out what we want (don't expect us to help you by explaining what we want, we expect you to know this through telepathy) and give us the right gift, do not expect smiles and thanks. We need to make a scene. Instead, we will remark,

"I see you finally got it right. It does not really make up for all the years you got it wrong does it?"

You can never win when it comes to providing us with gifts. We will always want to put you down no matter what you have done and irrespective of the effort and expense that you have gone to. We will always be unsatisfied and this will manifest in us giving you a dressing down in front of everyone at the party, or storming out of the venue at some sleight. Every year you will hear the same stinging accusation ringing in your ears,

"You've ruined my birthday. Again."

When it comes to your birthday the position is just as bad. We will routinely pretend to forget about it. Do not be fooled by our repeated apparent memory lapses. We have minds that remember everything and our powers of recall are spectacular. We know your birthday is on the horizon and with most things with us it generates two reactions. On the one hand we resent the forthcoming anniversary because it is a day geared towards the individual, namely you. It is not about us and we cannot stand that. It is rare that you ever allow the spotlight to be shone on you (by now you are so used to having to point it at us, you give up on it ever being fixed on you) but you do hold out the futile notion that it might still be done on your birthday, of all days. We find this galling. This is a day that will be about you and thus where will we get our fuel? Its approach generates dread and horror inside of us.

Conversely, we relish your birthday because we know, despite every previous disappointment, you still hold out hope that this year it might just be different. You pray to your own personal god that please, just for one, the day can pass without incident and you can enjoy yourself. You are not particularly bothered about doing anything special, perhaps a meal out somewhere and the gift need not be expensive, just so long as it exhibits that some kind of thought has gone into it. Your thoughts are based on hope as opposed to expectation. It will not be different because we need to spoil it; we need to make you feel upset and demeaned. To achieve this there are various things that we will do on your birthday.

1.      We forget about it completely. If you mention at 6pm that evening that it is your birthday we will lash out at you by explaining how busy we have been at work or that there has been some other pressing matter which means that it has slipped our minds. We deliberately forget about it and we will not countenance you criticising our omission.

2.      We organise something lavish but we know it is not something you will actually like. As usual, you put a brave face on it and fix a rigid smile to your face. We know what you are really thinking because we know it is not something you like. In fact, it is more likely that we have organised something that we enjoy. We do this so that everyone else can see what a grand and delightful gesture we have made and we drink in his or her admiration. It also enables us to poke at you repeatedly suggesting that you don't like it. We are goading you into making a tiny admission that it is not quite what you expected and then we erupt in self-indignant fury as we castigate you for being ungrateful after all the effort we have gone to.

3.      We buy some token gesture and point out that your 43rd birthday is not really something to celebrate is it? It is hardly a milestone. We then use this to remark on your advancing years and point out your various flaws.

4.    We organise a lovely birthday for you but spoil it by turning the spotlight back onto ourselves. We turn up late, we flirt with a guest or we manufacture some drama so that everyone is looking at us and not you. We complain at waiters when there is a family meal out, when there is not actual need to do so. We want to make a scene and wrench the spotlight back over to us.

5.    We remember your birthday and spend it doing what you want and we are pleasant to you until early evening when we deliberately pick a fight with you over absolutely nothing. The fuel we gain from this behaviour is all the sweeter as we have built you up, your guarded behaviour has melted away as we appear to have done everything that pleases you. We are waiting. We are waiting for you to feel good and happy and then we will cast you down so your emotional reaction is all the more heightened.

This behaviour is not just reserved for your birthday although we enjoy ruining your birthday the most. We do this with the birthdays of our children, friends and family. We hate it being about someone else and we hate seeing him or her being happy. In our world, nobody else is allowed a birthday and we believe that every day is our birthday and everyone should recognise that and act accordingly.

We know that you would rather your birthday be erased from the calendar. It is always a horrible day in one form or another and you would rather it not take place. We put a big red ring around it in the calendar in our mind and scribble next to the day the words, "Special Fuel Day."

## 24 Expect Remorse

We do not engage in showing remorse. We know how to say sorry. We should do because we hear you say it often enough. We never feel sorry for anything. Why should we? We never do anything wrong. Everything is always somebody else's fault, usually yours. In line with our sense of entitlement we are allowed to do as we please. Since that is the case, how can anything ever be our fault? When you demand that we apologise you offend us considerably. This is for several reasons.

1.      Who are you to expect us to apologise? You are inferior to us and you do what we want. It is not the other way around.

2.      An apology is an admission of wrongdoing. In case you somehow missed it, we do not do anything wrong.

3.      Remorse is exhibiting weakness. We are not weak. You are.

4.      You are being assertive. We do not like that as it threatens our control over you. We must have compliance. If we do not, we run the risk of losing fuel.

5.      If you expect us to apologise in front of others you will have a long wait. We must never lose face. What you can expect from us is a savage reaction behind closed doors for you having the audacity to try to embarrass us in this way.

We are genuinely baffled when you suggest to us that we ought to be sorry for something that has happened. It just does not compute with us. The reason for this is that to show remorse we understand that one has to understand how the other person has been hurt or affected in some way. As I have already explained and doubtless will need to explain again later, we have no time available to be thinking about how others may be affected by what we do. Even if we did, we lack the capacity to understand the feelings of others, as we have not been designed in such a way. This empathic approach has been denied to us. We give thanks that that is the case because we see exactly what happens to such people. They get dragged into a life of servitude to our need to acquire fuel. We shudder to think that that could actually happen to us.

Remorse is an important state to you. As an empathic individual you have no difficulty in apologising and expressing your regret for something that has happened or for something that you may have done (or failed to have done). You regard this as an integral part of being a well-adjusted individual. We know this because we have heard you speak about this on many occasions. We know that you understand the concept of remorse because you are able to place yourself in the other person's shoes. If you ever respond to somebody in a short-tempered fashion and they protest, you either know what it feels like (because you have experienced it yourself - something which has certainly happened when you have been entangled with our kind) or you are capable of working out how it must feel because of your naturally ability to express empathy. As a consequence of this, you expect us to be able to express remorse also. You expect this attribute of other people and it confuses you to find that we are incapable of doing so. You will fall into the trap of trying to demonstrate what we have done wrong (see trying to reason with us above) in order to then reach a state of remorse. All you are doing is giving yourself a mountain to climb and then when you think you have reached the peak; another mountain is revealed beyond the first. Oh and we are pulling on your rope trying to wrench you from the mountainside as you try to climb.

Not only are we incapable of feeling remorse and that we maintain adamantly that we have nothing to apologise for because we do nothing wrong, there is a further reason for our failure to ever express remorse. The majority of the time you want us to apologise and show sorrow for the horrible things that we have done to other people and mainly you. In our minds you are asking us to apologise for breathing. Why is that? You need to breathe to survive. We do as well but we also need to behave in this unpleasant way to survive. Our nasty treatment of you, the silences, the manipulation and the intimidation are all our methods of keeping you under control and providing us with fuel. We have to do it. Accordingly, by expecting us to show remorse for these behaviours you are expecting us to apologise for a fundamental and necessary action that in our world is akin to the need to eat, breathe, drink and sleep.

You would never contemplate saying sorry for having spent eight hours asleep would you? That is why we do not consider there is any need for us to apologise for this basic requirement to securing our existence. You point out however that your need for sleep does not harm someone else. You must sleep otherwise your will become fatigued, exhausted and ultimately ill. Going to sleep is not an act, which causes a consequence to somebody else whereas our bullying behaviour affects others. Your analysis appears correct except that we do not recognise you as someone else, someone separate and distinct from us. You are an extension and the harm that you may suffer from our necessary behaviour is just part of the equation. It is a by-product of a process, like exhaust fumes from an engine. Those fumes pollute and poison, much in the way that our behaviour is described but the engine must still run in the same way that our behaviours must take place if we are to survive. The necessity of this and our failure to regard you as a separate entity means that we cannot see any valid reason (even if we were capable of expressing it) for being remorseful about our conduct.

The only occasion when you will find us expressing some kind of remorse is when it suits our purposes. You must be aware that this expression is false. It is yet again a learned behaviour. We even hate to pretend to be remorseful because it smacks so much of weakness and that is something that we abhor. We will use it however when we sense that it is needed to avoid something worse from happening to us. This is usually the threat that we are about to lose a supply of fuel. If we recognise that you are going to leave us, we will put on our most contrite of appearances (whilst stifling our sniggers) and issue a mealy-mouthed apology for our behaviour. We will not actually be considering what that behaviour is because we are too focussed on ensuring that this ruse works and we prevent you from leaving us. We do not give any consideration to the supposed error of our ways. We do not listen to the lecture that you are giving us, your emphasis on changing and improving or whatever other sanctimonious drivel you are spouting, we just want you to accept our apology and remain as a source of fuel. Notice how we never appear sorry or apologetic when we do not stand to lose something. Pay attention to

119

how suddenly we can deploy our expression of contrition. Only yesterday we had been subjecting you to silent treatment and displaying our customary haughtiness towards you. Today you pack a suitcase and appear to be leaving us so we immediately realise we are in the Last Chance Saloon and decide that a display of false remorse is what is required. Our ability to switch from such unpleasant treatment to issuing a supposed apology is a clear indicator of the falsity of our sorrow. If we truly meant that we are sorry, we would not have been behaving in the way we did in the first place.

Keep in mind the number of times that we have supposedly expressed remorse and then repeated the behaviour. Do you find yourself thinking that you have experienced this before? Do you say to yourself that you have heard our apologies previously and you are going to leave and this time you mean it? Those are clear signs to you that we are leading you on a merry dance with this further form of manipulation. We know that deep down you do not want to go. We have deployed a variety of means to keep you hooked and we know that all you want is to hear us apologise. You truly believe that deep down inside of us there is some good and by saying sorry we are letting this rise to the surface. You are a good person and your worldview is that other people must be good as well, even those who appear to act to the contrary most of the time. Your view is entirely understandable given the type of person that you are but you are wasting your time if you ever expect a heart felt and meaningful expression of remorse from us.

You will however fall for our empty apology. Once we see you nod and accept what we have said we feel the relief and then a surge of power.

Our manipulation of you has worked again. There is every chance that what we have just falsely apologised for, we will go and do again within 24 hours. That is our way of maintaining power and also our method of sticking two fingers up at you.

Do not expect sorrow or remorse from us. It will not happen.

## 25 Expect to Enjoy Holidays

For those fortunate enough to enjoy an annual holiday or vacation, or possibly be in the position to travel more than once a year, that break from life's routines is a pleasant experience. Be it the chance to feel a hot sun on your back for a fortnight rather than a day, an opportunity to show off your prowess on the ski slope or scuba diving around a reef or strolling through a place of fascinating historical interest, the chance to go somewhere else is valued by many, many people. Lots of people plan their holidays well in advance giving them something to look forward to. They have some light at the end of the tunnel after the long weeks of work or caring for children, or both. There is the excitement perhaps of going to meet old friends who have moved to another country or continent, the chance to sample exotic cuisines, learn new customs and conventions and perhaps even try out your language skills. The holiday is regarded by many as an essential item in the cycle of life.

For those of you entangled with our kind a holiday perhaps holds the promise of some respite from the draining behaviour that you have been subjected to. It may be the case that you have booked a return to a sun-kissed beach, which we frolicked on during the seduction phase, and you (wrongly) think that by returning some of the magic of that golden period can be re-captured. It is not going to happen. You will not be living any stresses at the airport gate. You will not find a new lease life staring into the clear blue sea. Inspiration and invigoration will not rise from the

Roman ruins you stroll around. Our behaviour will continue and will actually be worse.

There are several reasons for this. First of all, your heightened sense of expectation on knowing you are going on holiday, which is ordinarily such an enjoyable experience, means that when it crashes (and it will) the fall will be hard. You should be recognising by now that we like to throw you into the abyss but we prefer to do so from the mountaintop. Your gloom and dejection is magnified if we do it amidst the supposed enjoyment of a holiday.

Secondly, holidays require preparation. There is the selection of the place to visit, the booking of flights, transport, accommodation and so on. The packing in readiness for the holiday which may range from a few suitcases to mobilising a small army if family are involved in say an extensive camping trip. I expand on this in greater detail below, but do not expect us to pull our weight in helping with these preparations. You will be left to do it yourself which will foster resentment and stress. Hopefully you will articulate this towards us, which will give us a pleasant dose of fuel and also the basis for blaming you in some way. Don't you just love that simmering silence tension on the drive to the airport? No? We certainly do.

Thirdly, the change of environment both alarms and excites us. It concerns us as we are being taken away from familiar circumstances (familiarity means low energy expenditure) and moreover we may be away from other sources of fuel. The person we have been conducting an affair with is now not somebody we are able to go and see. Our coterie of admirers has been taken away from us for a fortnight. Our simpering secretary is not able to fuel our ego every week day morning as he or she once did. The cessation of so many providers of fuel causes anxiety and concern to us. Add to this the risk that we may find ourselves technologically impaired or, heaven forbid, even without the use of the Internet or a mobile phone and we will feel cut adrift. The contemplation of such a horrific state of affairs will often cause us to argue against going anywhere. If you have managed to book somewhere there is little doubt that we will have protested about it and we will continue to berate you for doing something that we did not want to. Of course, we have no consideration for you wanting and needing a break.

By removing us from our natural habitat you provide us with something by which we can attack and criticise you. This helps address some of the enforced fuel deficit. It also provides us with the exciting opportunity to find new fuel. All of these new people who are at the resort, campsite, beach or on the cruise ship. Do not expect to spend a lot of time with us on a holiday. What time we have to spend together we will use to devalue you. The rest of the time we will be engaged in pursuing and obtaining different sources of fuel. We will be flirting with new prospects in the bar or at the pool. We may book in for some extra ski-ing lessons because we find the instructor attractive and amenable to our overtures. We will make new friends, using our irrepressible charm in order to win them over (just as we do with everyone new that we meet).

There is virgin territory to be conquered. New enraptured faces to hang on to our outlandish tales. Since we are on holiday we will boast of other places that we have gone to, we will exaggerate out domestic situation since they will never know to the contrary. Our car becomes faster and more expensive, the house has tripled in size and value and our form of employment has taken on a shinier lustre as we ramp up its importance. It feels fantastic to flex our boastful muscles and impress all these people. The lady who swims at 8am each morning, the pool attendant, the head barman, the chalet maid, the owner of the campsite, the crèche attendant and the ship's captain. All these people who have never been able to admire our brilliance before and now we have the chance to let it shine for them. If we had any decency, we would thank you for allowing us to embrace all these new and untapped sources of fuel but when did we ever express any gratitude? Or show a shred of decency for that matter?

You will be left behind in our wake. We will often disappear and when we saunter back after a day flirting with half a dozen people to be asked where have we been, we will launch an attack against you. We will explain we were letting you relax and it is our holiday too.

"It is not all about you, "we will declare without any sense of irony.

As you try and let the stress of the preparation for the holiday leave your body, we will rekindle it by spoiling those moments we spend together. We will brag in front of you and you dare not contradict what we say for fear of our reaction. We will incessantly talk about the marvellous new people we have met and how they admire and adore us. Without any concern we will flirt with people in front of you.

All you can expect of a holiday with us is that you will be demeaned and then left alone. As you lie on your sun lounge looking around the pools at the happy families and devoted couples you will feel lonely and unhappy. The only solace you might find is hoping that the shark fishing trip we decided to go on without you results in us falling into the sea and being eaten alive.

## 26 Ask Us What We Are Thinking

It is both a blessing and a curse for you to have to know what people are thinking and feeling. The uncharitable might label you as nosey. You do it because you like to be able to know this to enable you to respond in the most constructive and pleasant fashion. If someone is having a difficult day and is plagued with unpleasant thoughts, you want to know about it. You can then offer words of encouragement and support. Should someone be in a good mood you are pleased for him or her and want to be able to share in that positive experience.

When your kind become ensnared by us you have no or little understanding of what is happening. You need to seek out answers in order to fathom out why we are behaving as we are. Our actions and words lack logic and this flies contrary to the way you operate. Not only do you need to understand why we are doing what we are doing, you also want to be able to help.

"How can I help you if you do not tell me what it is that is wrong?"

"If you do not talk to me, I cannot help you and I want to help you."

"Why won't you tell me what the problem is? If you do, I am sure we can work it out."

"Keeping it to yourself is not going to help. A problem shared and all that."

Do you recognise those comments and questions?

We won't tell you what we are thinking. First of all, we want you to guess. We love to play games and having you try to work out what is going on in our minds is a game we do like to indulge in. Keeping you guessing means you keep paying us attention and that means fuel. Secondly, this will ensure you remain in a state of confusion. We do not want you to work our why we behave as we do and we do not want you to know what is going on in our heads. You remain confused and bewildered and that means we are able to exert our control over you for longer. By keeping you confused, we heighten your anxiety, which in turn will tire you out. This will result in your coping mechanisms becoming depleted and as a consequence you will become more malleable to our manipulative conduct.

Thirdly, we are of the firm opinion that you should already know what we are thinking. Yes, I realise this is contradictory to our desire to have you know what is going in our minds, but we are a myriad of contradictions because we are entitled to be this way. You should know what we want before we even want it. You should be anticipating our needs and requirements. If you fail to do so, then you must not love us. That is the conclusion that we reach. We think that you cannot be bothered to consider our needs and we regard your behaviour as being contrary to our well being. It is of no consequence to us that you do not have telepathic powers, that we do not tell you what we are thinking about or what we want, you are expected to know. This is because as an innately superior person our needs should be anticipated and met. Since you are beneath us, this is the role to which you have been assigned and you should deliver. Do not bleat to us about the impossibility of your task and how we do not help you fathom out what we want, we have much more important matters to attend to. You are becoming a distraction and you risk incurring our wrath.

Fourthly, we love to be regarded as enigmatic. By creating this appearance of depth we feel powerful and god-like. Our kind is shallow and base creatures and depth is something beyond our grasp although we covet it. In order to fabricate that sense of depth we attempt to create an air of mystery about us. Do not disturb us as we sit staring out of the window looking across the view. We want you thinking that we are embroiled in deep and philosophical considerations. We can see you from the corner of your eye looking on in admiration.

"He seems so lost in thought, it must be something important."

"I wonder what mammoth principles he is grappling with right now?"

"If only I could equal what is going on in the great mind right now."

This is what we tell ourselves that you are thinking as you look at us. Yes, we are great, yes we are masters of deep contemplation and such is the weight of our thoughts that you will not be able to carry them. Do not even try to do that. Do not ask what we are thinking about, you cannot possibly understand. We do not want you to shatter the illusion that we are creating that we are people of substance and engaged in wrestling with thoughts beyond your comprehension.

Finally, and ultimately, we do not want you to ask us what we are thinking because we do not want to tell you what is actually running through our minds. We do not want to divulge the dark thoughts that course through our consciousness. That would give the game away. We do not want you to realise that our thoughts actually operate on a fairly limited level. Yes, we are articulate, knowledgeable and well read but all we do then is regurgitate what we have learned. I have told you about our formidable powers of recall. We are experts at copying and absorbing as we take on the personas and personalities as others. We hijack ideas and pass them off as our own, we can repeat that wonderful part of Hamlet's soliloquy and we will sing all the verses of a particularly beautiful song but we are but a magpie. We dart in and steal from others and pretend that the pilfered item is ours.

The only real creative thoughts that we engage in are associated with one thing; the acquisition of fuel. Where can we get it from next? How will we do it? What will the best way to achieve it? Who can we secure it from and how much? What methods should we engage to bring about the flow of delicious, sweet, sweet fuel?

What are we thinking? We are devising, planning and plotting. We are constructing lies and fallacies to obtain our fuel. We are building more of our fictitious world and generating more of our fantasy. Our Machiavellian minds are engrossed in the dark and the nefarious. These considerations revolve around seducing you and others, our schemes envelope the savage devaluing of you, casting you down from the pedestal and subjecting you to our dark arts. Do not ask what we are thinking. We won't say for the reasons outlined above and in truth, do you really want to know what is going on inside our evil minds?

## 27 Expect Us to Buy You Gifts

We do not buy you gifts. Hold on, we hear you say, what about all those presents that came our way at the beginning of our relationship? We were showered with tokens of affection ranging from the small and thoughtful to the extravagant. Barely a day went by without some kind of present being delivered by a courier or produced from behind our back to give to you with a smile and a flourish. From the flowers to the jewellery, from the copious bottles of fine wine and champagne to the multitude of shoes and accessories, we festooned you with our largesse. Every conceivable material formed part of our avalanche of generosity. Leather, slate, cotton, gold, diamond, plastic, aluminium, wax, wood, paper, glass and sapphire were those items amongst the many that we sourced and sent to you. Artisans, manufacturers and creators shaped and moulded beautiful items by which you dazzled you, pulling you closer so our hooks could ensnare you. At times you barely hard time to open them all before the next set of gifts arrived. What about all of that?

Those were not gifts bought by us. They were bribes and we did not buy them. Someone else paid for them. In some instances, we used the financial resources of others to enable us to obtain all of these material items. We are not going to use our own money for that purpose, not when there are others who can so easily be relied on to do this for us. From time to time we would borrow money from others and used it to impress you, spending beyond our means although you had no idea of this.

131

On other occasions the credit of an outgoing interest would be utilised to provide an investment in the twisted opportunity that you presented to me. Those who parted with their own financial resources will have been duped into doing so. Coerced by false promises of repayment or in the vain hope that by appeasing me using cold, hard currency it might halt my cold, hard treatment of them. Where sometimes we may have appropriated the resources of others to support our extravaganza in other instances the payment would come from you in due course. We never do something for nothing. Everything has its price and you end up paying dearly for what really are little more than trinkets.

Ask those who received the dizzying array of flattering gifts whether they were worth the twenty years of abuse they have suffered? The answer will be a resounding no. The gifts you received during the seduction phase were bribes. Inducements for you to leave your reason behind as you became entranced by the sparkling of gems, the gleam of precious metals, the cool and smooth allure of electronic gadgets, the scent of the interior of a new vehicle, the crisp sensation of a beautiful dress as you held it against you. Those bribes were financed by others and by your own emotional costs, which had yet to be extracted.

Once the bribes achieved their purpose then the display of extravagance concluded. No longer did we bring your flowers whereas once upon a time we always did so on a Friday. The surprise presents dried up. The tap was swiftly turned off. We had no need to bombard you with such finery as you had fallen under our spell. We no longer wanted to apply our energies to thinking of the shiny and seductive and thus we stopped.

As an alternative, the expectancy we created by our outlandish behaviour was then used against you.

"Don't you think you have had enough from me?"

"After all the things you have had from me and you begrudge me buying this one thing?"

"You really are selfish. When I think about everything I have bought for you."

"You don't need anything else, I have given you everything you could possibly ever need."

Should you persist in wanting tokens of material affection then this will mean we have to use our own resources. We will not do this. We will argue against any such expenditure even though we will continue to make lavish purchases for ourselves. We will look to get you to foot the bill (and quite probably you are now doing so for our campaign of bribery to our next victim) but we are loath to ever make payment ourselves. We feel no affection for you so why would we want to display this by buying you gifts? Why would we want to use up our financial resources on someone we now detest and whose continuing process annoys and offends us?

Attempt to make us account for this change in behaviour and we will go on the attack, labelling you a mercenary and self-centred. It will form the basis for our character assassinations of you. It will also enable us to go with the begging bowl to others. We will cry about the demands you are making on us in order to extract money from other people. We will say we need to purchase a new car for you otherwise you will leave.

People will still fall for this and loan us money towards such a purchase. No car will ever be bought. We will pocket the donation (for that is how we see it) and use it for our own use, most typically to fund one or more of our addictions.

With many things that we do, we like to expose you to it first so you become reliant and addicted to the pleasure associated with it. We then remove it brutally and swiftly so that the pain and confusion caused to you is at a maximum. This provides us with a tremendous sense of satisfaction. You do not deserve any gifts. You are not worthy of them in our view. It just reinforces our sense that you are an inferior parasite, leeching off our previous generosity both materially and emotionally. All of this is designed to keep you under our control, confused and bewildered as we look to make you count the cost of becoming entangled with us.

We do not buy you gifts. We are securing an investment in our false creation and nobody leaves without paying.

## 28 Criticise Us

To criticise me is to unleash my rage.

You are not allowed to criticise our kind because: -

1.    We are always right;

2.    We are above criticism;

3.    Our superiority means that criticism is not applicable to us;

4.    You are in no position to judge us since you are beneath us; and

5.    It is far too painful for us to endure.

You are familiar now with our superiority and the maintenance of our immunity to any form of criticism, sleight or slur. You have endured our daily reinforcement of your position of inferiority and you are not surprised by our haughty rejection of your adverse comments about us.

Nobody likes to be criticised. Many people perpetuate the myth that they are open to constructive criticism. That is nonsense. Everybody feels wounded when what he or she have done or said is criticised in some way. Whether the critic couches the comment in a euphemistic fashion or whether they dismantle the subject in a withering torrent of contempt, the recipient does not like it. People are programmed to recoil instinctively. Their sense of pride and achievement has been impugned and the criticism, no matter how well intentioned, pains us. People are likely to enter into a defensive mode in order to protect themselves. We have noticed that you and others tend to deny the criticism and try and remove yourselves from the comments that are being made. You do not like it. Now imagine how it feels when we are being criticised. I can wager you will do your best to envisage that visceral sense of injury because you are very good at putting yourself in the place of others.

When we are criticised our constructed world begins to fall apart. The structure we have created comes under attack because it is built on a foundation that we are impervious to such denigrating remarks. We are the best of everything. As I have explained above in respect of how you should not try to understand us, we are those glittering skyscrapers that have been constructed to reach the sun and to enable us to commune with God. Higher and taller than anything else, we are a tribute to the astonishing feats of engineering that has enabled our creation to rise upwards. Fashioned from everything we desire around us; it is a marvellous edifice. Gleaming glass panes that reflect as the spire soars up in to the firmament. The metal beams and brickwork held in place with the rivets of admiration and mortar of adoration. To gaze upon our cathedral is to be astonished at the breath taking grandeur of this architectural behemoth.

Yet for all its magnificence the tiniest remark that questions our brilliance sends a crack from the base of our tower. It runs upwards, the fracture increasing in length and width as it becomes a fissure and the first shards shear away to plummet to the ground. The earth begins to shake, threatening to demolish this house of cards. The metal begins to buckle, the rivets popping out with each syllable of criticism that is sent our way. When you criticise us, our world begins to crumble. We cannot stand to watch this happen as it pains us. The sensation is agonising. You may regard your comment as minor in nature and couched in the least offensive manner you could think of, but it not that way to us. You might as well have taken a wrecking ball to what we have made as your words feel vicious and harsh to us.

I detail below two situations that have generated this outcome. One is based on our tower never having been subjected to any kind of testing environment before and as a consequence it is ill equipped to deal with the reality of the world. This tower although glorious and beautiful was built in a cocoon and once it became exposed to reality, it is found to be wanting. The second type of tower is built on imaginary foundations in order to impress those who have always doubter the builder's capabilities. Those foundations cannot sustain the edifice.

You are demolishing our world but you are also taking us back to our childhoods. We know better than most how effective a sharp jolt back to childhood can be in evoking powerful emotions, usually of a negative nature. We use this technique regularly ourselves by learning about some childhood vulnerability or trauma of yours and thereafter exploiting it. By causing you to return to that terrible moment in an instant we wield tremendous power over you. With much that we do, we like to dole it out but we are ill equipped in terms of coping with it ourselves.

When we were children we invariably fell into one of two camps. In the first we were the golden children, those who were held up as shining examples of brilliance and achievement. Everything we did was praised; everything we turned our hand to was marvelled at and declared fantastic. We thrived on this daily praise and grew accustomed to it. Not only did this prove formative in our unshakeable belief that we are special and magnificent, it also meant that we became ill equipped when someone eventually did criticise us. All through our formative years we were showered with admiration and praise. We bathed in a golden light. Nothing we ever did was wrong or incorrect. Years later, should someone and in particular you, criticise us, not only can we not process that it is happening, we have no internal defence by which we can manage it. We are the illusion believers. Thus, those of us who were the golden children find criticism intensely damaging and hurtful. I know this only too well.

I am also aware, through my dealings with certain relatives of mine, that there are those who fall into a second camp. This is the place where as children they faced a huge level of expectation and they failed to live up to it. These are the illusion creators. Impossibly high standards had been set for them with every facet of their lives and no matter how hard they tried, studied, ran, behaved and applied themselves it was never, ever enough. Each time they thought that they had secured the required grade, the goalposts were moved and with it the scathing criticism. They were told they should have been better, they should have achieved this, they ought to have done that and overall why could they not be more like me? This caused them to build an idea of what they should be in order to rise above the childhood castigation. It worked because it appeased those who lacked substance themselves and thus that child kept on building this idea, the tower on the poor foundation, over and over, expecting it to be the answer to all the demands made of it. This construction cannot withstand criticism. At best, it tries to shield by illusion but when those casting the criticism operate in reality and they are of substance, their weighty words shatter this idea in an instant and cause it to come crashing down.

When you criticise the golden child you are offending our childhood right to be superior and impregnable. When you criticise the illusion creators you remind them of those crushing words that they heard in their formative years. In each instance the pain is horrendous. There is only one way we know to remove that pain. Create more pain; yours. Your criticism of us will unleash our narcissistic rage and we will become abusive. The extent of this abuse need not be commensurate with the level of sleight that has been sent out way. We are flailing our fists, either literally or figuratively, in a desperate and sudden bid to hurt you and thus make our own pain stop. We need to bludgeon you; we need to gut you and make you bleed in order for us to regain our sense of power and superiority. This rage rebuilds our respective tower. We believe in the illusion again or we create the illusion again. Either way our tower becomes restored as we land blow after blow on you. You only have yourself to blame for this. You really ought to know better than to criticise us. By attacking you we are invalidating you. You do not matter, you are inconsequential and beneath us. What you have said by way of criticism cannot matter for you have no bearing any more. Your disapproval of us by reason of this criticism stings so deeply that we must attack you and often in the most brutal fashion.

Do not criticise us. You will regret it more than we will.

# 29 Flirt in front of us

We are allowed to flirt. You are not. Such a contradiction should come as no surprise to you by now. We use flirtation to draw our victims into our web and thereafter as a mild form of triangulation to provoke an emotional reaction from those we are meant to be to commit to. It is entirely permissible for us to be flirtatious, although I do not actually regard it as such conduct. I see it as being friendly, taking an interest in people and fulfilling my role as someone that people are naturally drawn to. As I have had to tell jealous partners in the past, I cannot help being popular and if you want to be remain with me, you will need to get used to it. Naturally, I know what I am doing with the choice words, carefully gauged tactile gestures and suggestive comments. I am gathering fuel from the individual who is now caught in the glare of my sizzling laser beams, pinned to the spot by my flattering comments and witty badinage. All the while we can sense you glowering nearby, not daring to say anything or do anything to interrupt our display and more importantly our feeding on this fuel, but sufficiently irritated to provide us with another fuel line. It is marvellous.

I have seen some of you decide that the best way to deal with us is to use our own behaviour against us. Admittedly, that can work with some of our manipulative ways. It usually results in us shutting off that particular technique and opening up a different front. Do not make the mistake of flirting in front of us however. You are giving us the green light to go on the attack. Should you do this, you have cut off a supply of fuel to us. You are not reacting to our treatment of you, as we desire, by you becoming jealous and silently raging in a corner. Instead you are being assertive and you are challenging our superiority. This is not permitted. Furthermore, you are making us look foolish in front of other people. Worst of all, you are telling the recipient of your flirtation that you are a free agent. You are not. You belong to us. You are our property. You are our appliance. You do not work for anyone other than us. You are telling us that we are not good enough and that you have found somebody better than us. We cannot comprehend that being the case. Nobody is better than us. Have you forgotten all the wonderful things that we did for you when we were seducing you? Have you cast to one side all the magnificent gestures and words that we used? How dare you throw all of that back in our faces? You are selfish, slutty and you disgust us.

This attack against us is on several fronts.

1.      The removal of fuel;

2.      The challenge to our superiority;

3.      You are diminishing our standing.

None of this can be deemed as acceptable. You should have grasped that we regularly adopt double standards. What we do is fine but you must not do it and we will stand and berate you about your conduct having behaved exactly the same way only moments earlier and not bat an eyelid at our outrageous hypocrisy. We do not like it when people use our tools against us. We fashioned those tool, you did not.

If you are fortunate, we will log your transgression and then subject you to retribution once we are home. It is likely we will take steps to record your behaviour. You may notice this but emboldened by your assertive behaviour and also we can see you are enjoying the reaction you are getting from us (who is displaying the narcissistic tendencies now eh?) you continue with the behaviour and increase it. We will make a note of what you are doing in accurate detail in our minds and ally it with some footage. Notwithstanding the times you have replayed our own conduct back to us, which we have denied and avoided, we will do the same to you. We will also make a great show of exhibiting it to other people to underline what a horrible person you are and your treatment of us is despicable. We will then exact our revenge against you behind closed doors and let you know just how mightily you have offended us.

In certain instances, the indignant fury that you unleash in us by flirting with somebody offends us to such a degree that we lose control there and then. We fly into a rage and haul you away from the object of your affections. Should they try and intervene they will also be subjected to our anger and more than likely physically. We will dress you down in front of everyone else and it is highly likely we will force you to leave early, our nasty insults echoing behind as we leave the venue. By this point we care little for what people might think about our outburst, we are comforted by the fact that we know it is your fault. Should anyone raise our explosion with us we will explain how it was your fault that we ended up doing this, that anybody else would have done the same in such a situation and invite them to speak to you, as you are the real villain of the piece, not us.

Your attempts to deflect blame back onto us will not work. Even though we routinely flirt with people that of course if our birthright. We are masters at it and it is a tool of our trade. You are not permitted to copy us. You must know your place. Trying to use one of our methods against us is not wise move and will have very definitely unpleasant consequences for you.

# 30 Expect Us to Pull Our Weight

The world owes us a living and yet the world is not enough for us. We are creatures of economy. We hate to use our own resources at all and certainly not for others. When we seduce you none of the effort we apply is for your benefit. It is not undertaken to provide you with any comfort or pleasure. The fact that this happens is utterly incidental to our stated aim of bringing you under our spell. If there was another way this could be achieved, one where you did not feel loved, happy and elated we would take it. Especially if that alternative method proved to be even more efficient.

The resources we dedicate are to further our own aims. Every step we take is designed to bring about fuel for us and the easier this can be achieved, so much the better. This approach to behaving in a tight and mean fisted way, combined with the fact we have no time or energy to dedicate to anybody else because we are fixated with getting our fix means that you cannot expect us to pull our weight.

A number of our brethren do not work. Why bother with that when you can be relied on to bring home the money. Our time is much better applied to chasing the neighbour, playing video games, lying in bed sleeping and lying to our tangled web of social media playthings. Do not expect those stay at home narcissists to apply themselves to ensuring a smooth running household. How can they possibly do that when there are six fake internet dating profiles to attend to, facebook stalking to address and the coercing of nude selfies from naïve hangers on? No, you can do the laundry, clean the house and prepare the food when you return from work. Any attempt to berate us about our lack of contribution will result in the deployment of all our standard evasive behaviours before going on the attack. Have you still not learned to get on with it, keep your head down and keep quiet?

I, like many others of our kind, prefer to work. Well, I describe it as work; it is more a highly paid game of chess. The workplace provides me with so many opportunities to obtain fuel. From my secretary who I know is in love with me but dare not say so, to the competing assistants who are all vying for the oft promised but yet to be delivered promotion and then on to the other staff who I enjoy flirting with or setting against one another. Fortunately for me, through a combination of natural brilliance and astute gamesmanship I climbed the ladder in record time. I yanked off those above me and stamped on the fingers of those racing up behind me until I was without peer of competition. Once I reached my position of dominance I burned the ladder and became impregnable.

The other week I sat in my corner office admiring the view across the city and marvelling at how I spend more time avoiding doing any work than actually doing work. My time is spent ensuring others deliver whilst at the same time maintaining my sources of work-based fuel. I achieve all of this whilst extracting a significant profit share from the business. I think you will agree that that is rather impressive. I never pull my weight at work. I do not have to. I have positioned myself to ensure that there is always somebody else who can be asked (or made if really necessary) to do what needs to be done. I don't get my hands dirty. As I

146

advanced I always ensured I dodged the difficult assignments, dragging a competitor into the line of fire. My natural charm ensured that I had the higher-ups on my side from early on. Plus, my natural ability to extract information and gather intelligence ensured I had some insurance when it came to three of my bosses. They have gone now, shuffled sideways or out of the business once their use had expired or rather when their lack of usefulness had been pointed out to those even higher. Efficiency savings mean more profit and I am the king of efficiency.

From my perspective as a high functioning narcissist, the fact I achieve so much in the workplace means that I do not engage in the mundane activities in the household. I never have. Those types of things are for the help or for you. Those who I deigned to live with knew not to complain about their requirement to attend to domestic chores. Not if they wanted to enjoy the lifestyle that I provided. Several of them were shallow creatures. I put them through some; let's say challenging behaviour but they stuck around. They valued the expensive and the shiny over their souls. Their choice and they paid for it.

Whether you are involved with a superstar like me, a middle ranker salary man or the devious stay at home member of our club, it matters little. The outcome will always be the same. You do the lion's share of the legwork. You clean, launder, shop, childcare, entertain and of course run around after us. Do not expect in particular for us to play a meaningful role in the raising of children. They absorb too much attention away from us and are best avoided unless there is scope for some vicarious fuel to be gained from them. Claiming the credit for their achievements can be a lucrative little sideline from time to time, but more on that later on. We will always be able to find a reason why you should do this and not us. We will remind you of our contributions, find some other pressing matter we must attend to (which is another way of us saying we have to attend to securing some fuel) or just launch into an unnecessary attack to keep you in your place.

It would be a misnomer to label us as lazy. We are far from that. The mind is always racing as we devise fresh plots to obtain fuel, new ways to devalue you and additional excuses to deploy so we can maintain the status quo. We are always on the go. In fact, it is exhausting doing what we do. That permanent hunger has to be fed. This entire endeavour must of course be directed to our benefit and never anybody else. No matter what we promised in the golden period, irrespective of the false hope we give you when we claim we will help out more and make more of a contribution and despite the occasional spurts of help we may show in order to fulfil a grander design, you will never get us pulling our weight.

## 31 Compare Us to Others

"Nobody does it better, makes me feel sad for the rest." So sang Carly Simon in the theme to The Spy Who Loved Me. That could have been written about us. We are the best and the sooner you recognise and accept that so much the better. By acknowledging that you are fortunate enough to be involved with a high power such as us you will not only feel blessed but you will also save yourself much aggravation. You can take some pride in the fact that someone as brilliant chose somebody like you. Not everyone fits the bill in respect of our requirements and in doing so you are admitted to an exclusive membership. There is a heavy price to pay for being a member of this club (it is not our club, you are not good enough for that, but it is affiliated) and for many of you the price is too great. You ought to reflect though and consider that if you do, as we require, comply with our wishes and supply us with fuel then you can consider that you have done your job well and into the bargain you have been able to stand slightly behind (never alongside) some people as remarkable as us.

If you compare us to others, you will only experience bitterness as those other people will not be able to attain our greatness. Look around you. Consider the world leaders, the brilliant economists, sensational authors, outstanding actors and actresses, the remarkable directors, pioneering captains of business and peerless sports men and women. All of them possess single-mindedness, drive, ambition and a fearless appetite for success. They are all members of our club. The songwriters, the pop stars, the entertainers, television hosts and film moguls. They are all fully paid up to our club. The world needs these people. You want to be led; you want to be amused and entertained don't you? You want brilliance to shine in your direction, if only for a short while, to lift you out of your mundane existence? Of course you do. Not anybody can reach the top like these people. You have to be made of something special, something different. We have it. Not many do. Of course, not all members of our order make it to the top, there are after all so many slots to go around but the majority are occupied by our kind. It is nigh on impossible for anyone other than our type to reach those elevated positions. Don't believe me? Pick somebody famous, a leader in his or her field or at the top of their game and then apply the diagnostic material for our kind. Most of the boxes will be ticked.

If you persist in comparing us to others this will only lead to bitterness and jealousy as you cannot and nor can many others achieve where we get to. We are trying to spare you the wasted effort in telling you this (and naturally ensuring that you focus on something much more worthwhile, namely us). Accept that our kind is where we are and do not envy or bemoan that fact.

You must never compare us to others and suggest that we could be different or better or that we could change in some way. We find that hugely offensive. We are special and to be likened to somebody who will be evidently inferior to us will annoy us intensely. Why would we want to be like them when we are above them? We are content to acquire parts of other people for our own use though. We regard that as acceptable and something we must do to survive, but that is acquisition and it is not comparison. It is also based on what we choose to take for our purposes since we are best placed to judge what we need. You are not. We know you have an agenda. You fear our brilliance and by that you seek to do us harm. You want to weaken us by making us become like the weak. We worked your kind out a long time ago. You think you are so clever by suggesting that these are all good attributes that we should acquire.

"You should be more like John and show more patience."

"Take a leaf out of Jane's book and think before you speak. She is always considerate."

"Have you noticed how calm Eric always is? You might find it useful to do likewise."

"Why don't you do like Paula and think about someone else for a change other than yourself?"

You dress this up as meaning well but you come to us cloaking your intent. You want to sink a dagger between our shoulder blades and drain us of our strength by having us engage in behaviour, which can only bring about weakness and vulnerability. Patience? When did waiting around for something ever get anything done? Consideration? That means getting trampled in the rush as you let everyone else go first. Calm? Being soporific is hardly going to set the world alight is it? Think about others? I do that all the time. How much fuel can I get from him and her and them.

To compare us to others and suggest that we alter our ways to become more like them is purely a ploy to destabilise our control of you.

We have a slight sneaking admiration for your ingenuity. As ever, you dress everything up in the best of intentions, but we have the measure of you. We are the masters, not you. We are the verb not the object. We do, we are not done to. So, nice try Captain Empathy but this General is not going to be deposed.

Should you persist in this course of action we will have to take steps to remind you who is in charge and that means subjecting you to our methods of control It will not be pleasant, but conditioning a transgressor never is. The short, sharp shock is what is necessary to get you back in line and returning to your place in the scheme of things. Know your place. Recognise your superiors and all will be well. Save the comparisons to insurance websites.

## 32 Expect to Enjoy Christmas

"It's the most wonderful time of the year," so sang somebody who I do not recall about Christmas. No it is not. There is little doubt that the Grinch belonged to our club. We hate Christmas and that means that it is going to be awful for you as well. In fact, any kind of celebration will result in you dreading the day as it appears and you are walking on eggshells throughout the entirety of the day. What should be enjoyable for everyone becomes a nightmare and it is one of our deliberate creations.

The ghastliest thing about Christmas is the concept of giving. Don't get me wrong, if you want to engage in giving, be my guest, so long as it is towards me and nobody else. Do not expect me to reciprocate either. Christmas requires effort and we don't do effort. Writing Christmas cards, shopping for gifts (did you not read the chapter above about giving you gifts?), preparing food, visiting people, entertaining people and putting up with relatives for days on end. No thank you. If you want to put all the effort in to doing this, you can go ahead. In fact, I would rather you did so that I can come in and provide the final flourish to the Christmas tree or sail in and sit at the head of the table with all the food prepared and set out so I can engage in regaling all assembled with my anecdotes about how marvellous I am.

You might think that given some of the chapters above that I might see Christmas as an opportunity to identify and extract new forms of supply. This can occasionally happen but it is not the promise of potent fuel that you might expect. First and foremost, Christmas is for children and they are the black holes of fuel. I might attend somebody's party on Boxing Day and be engaged in amazing them with some of my standard tales as I aim to seduce them when some rug rat will appear and tug at my target's skirt. Her attention will switch to little Johnny and my efforts have dissipated as she goes off to find him a slice of cake or take him to the toilet. Some of the games where I hold centre stage at an adults' gathering become ineffectual as I am annoyingly upstaged by a precocious brat with their rendition of Silent Night causing cooing from those assembled. Alternatively, one of the youngsters attending decides to start crying and thus attention turns to him or her to try and placate and soothe the bawling child. That attention should be focussed on me, not him or her. I find it galling to say the least.

What troubles me considerably is the fixation with a fictional fat fellow in a red suit. Write a letter to Santa. Santa is watching so you had better be good. Visit one of Santa's helpers. Make some mince pies for him and leave them out. Stop going on about bloody Santa, he does not even exist. I exist but it is hard work trying to compete with Father Christmas. I become so infuriated with the fuss that is made about him and I have yet to work out a decent smear campaign that might bring him down, the jovial rotund chap seems impervious to a good character assassination. I am still working on that though.

I used to get a kick out of telling my younger siblings that Father Christmas did not exist causing them to cry. I still remember that warm feeling that would flow over me as I watched the tears flow from them. The red faces, scrunched up as I pointed out with hard fact after hard fact as to how he could not exist. I was always punished for this but it was worth it. People need to know the truth about certain things.

I think I dislike Christmas so much because it tends to usurp much of my abilities, not something I like to admit but there it is. I am about everything that is shiny and new, I dangle the glittering baubles in front of you to lead you by the nose into my fantasyland. What does Christmas do? It insists on having trees decked out in shiny baubles and bright lights. Houses are festooned with twinkling, glittering lights. Tinsel abounds and wreaths, stockings and garlands demand attention. The radio emits an incessant parade of festive songs; which people would rather listen to than my tales of excellence. The demands of preparation ensure people are too preoccupied with organising all of those things when they should be directing their attention to me. They are ringing friends, other family members and arranging visits. You spend your time saying how you have not seen people for so often and you then divert your attention to them. I have spent all year trying to keep you isolated and part from your networks and Christmas comes barging in ruining my entire endeavour.

I react the only way I know. With disdain, criticism and nastiness. I refuse to participate in activities, I will not help with the preparation, and I do my utmost to avoid having people visit unless I can be sure they will give me the fuel I demand. I am content to attend parties, especially if children are unlikely to be there, this provides me with some hope as I stalk the room sucking up fuel from every available source of admiration. I break gifts; I hide them and turn my nose up at them in order to prompt a reaction. I mess with the controls on the cooker in the hope of spoiling Christmas lunch so a scene develops. I do love the drama of an undercooked turkey. I will try and embrace your sister inappropriately under the mistletoe and then blame her for being drunk. I must admit that despite all my endeavours it is a difficult period to get through. You remain frighteningly cheerful at times and there is too much going on which detracts from the attention I want.

I hate Christmas and I will routinely do as much as I can to spoil it for you as well. You have to work hard to keep it on course. Sometimes it will work and sometimes it will not. There are occasions where the best I can hope for is to sit and sulk and make a mental note of all the things you do during this period that offend me and bring them up once your family have departed and no more friends will be calling round. Alone and cornered I can reassert my superiority and control. I won't enjoy Christmas so do not waste your time trying to make sure that I do and watch out, because I will be trying to derail it for you. Bah humbug!

## 33 Ditch Our Technology

Technology is a massive boon to our kind. It has given us an unprecedented reach. Our numbers are growing because of it, as I set out in the introduction. We have a fascination with technology for two reasons. Firstly, it enables us to rope in our victims and keep them where we want them. The use of technology allows us to learn lots about you before we even speak to your face. We use it to mine for information about you which we can then use to seduce you. It allows us to keep up a near incessant flow of compliments and declarations of love when we are love bombing you. Our seduction of you is like the outbreak of war. We drop a salvo of texts, launch a thousand e-mail love missiles and bombard you with telephone propaganda. We send in a legion of tweets, a battalion of snap chat pictures and a phalanx of instagramming. You have no option but to surrender to this blitzkrieg, which is all enabled and amplified by technology. During the relationship technology enables us to keep tabs on where you and what you are doing. We can send one blistering text to ruin your evening. Technology allows us to triangulate by posting pictures of attractive people we just happened to meet in a bar causing you to feel jealous and excluded. We even triangulate you with our technology. Have you seen how much time I spend with my smart phone as opposed to you? Technology allows us to deploy our much-loved tactic of intermittent reinforcement. We have subjected you to the bad, bad and worse of our behaviour and we sense you might have had enough. It is time to open the gates to heaven again for a few moments so we send you that loving text and you cling on again.

We know that people are hooked on getting validation. Think about when you post something on Facebook. How long do you wait before checking to see if you have received any comments or likes? How often do you keep referring to your 'phone or tablet to ascertain if the likes or comments have increased? How do you feel if nobody responds? How do you feel when somebody does respond? People are now conditioned to want that occasional reinforcement from something as banal as posting a picture. We know just how powerful it is to provide you with that intermittent feeling of being approved and validated in our relationship, especially after we have treated you in such a terrible fashion. Technology allows us to perform this step in an instant.

We love it because it allows us all manner of different ways to extend our tendrils and Hoover you back in again. We can find out where you are through your social media postings, send a variety of ways to contact you using technology and even up the ante by bugging your home and placing a GPS tracker no your vehicle.

The second reason we love technology is that most of it amounts to an inanimate object. We adore these items. Take the Ipad. Those cool, sleek lines with the delicious rounded corners. The smooth glass front with the defining border. The weight of it in our hand, the coldness of the silver rear section, which will gradually warm with use. The marvellous interface and efficiency of its layout. All of those are things that we admire. We are lovers of appliances. Press a button and it performs. That is what we want you to be. A pre-programmed appliance that churns out fuel when we press your buttons. Walking through the electronic section of a department store is heaven for us. All these beautiful designs, so elegant and clean. Row upon row of appliances that have been designed to deliver over and over again. Televisions, monitors, washing machines, coffee machines, tumble dryers, music systems, Ipods, Xboxes, Playstations, Pcs, tablets, smartphones even the humble toaster. Press a button and it does what it is designed to do. This represents to us the ultimate ideal. We want you to be that appliance. We want you to sit quietly and perform for us. We press the buttons and you deliver to us the fuel with the minimum of effort and exertion from us.

It is for these two reasons that we value technology over everything else. Should you ever remove or damage our technology expect our response to be one of fury. You may consider the tactic of switching off the wifi and hiding the router to be something that will cause us to stop spending everything evening on the internet as we flirt with virtual sources of fuel and trawl internet dating sites. All you will do by denying us that opportunity is to cause us to become angry. We will not recognise that we have spent every night for the last fortnight head dipped, staring at the screen and ignoring you. We have been busy working as we search for fuel and now you have undone all our hard work and denied us our precious resource. You should expect a vicious backlash.

Should you remove any of our technological tools we will go into frenzy as we try to find them. We need these items and will try to locate them and if not we will immediately seek out replacements before launching a tirade against you. You are dismantling our networks and interfering with something that does as it is told. Why can you not be like that? Damage our technology, be it on purpose or even accidentally and the anger will rise once again. We will lash out in fury at your desecration of what is holy to us. Whatever you do, you must not say,

"It is only a scratch."

"Look, it still works."

"Why are you making such a fuss over a computer?"

"You are married to that thing."

This is slanderous in the extreme and will only cause our anger to increase as you belittle the item that we covet and rely on. Technology helps us survive. It performs, as we want it to. We regard this as utopia. Whole rooms of technology quietly executing their tasks with maximum efficiency, controlled by us and delivering to us our fuel. You should copy this example and plug yourself in and continue to deliver the fuel that we demand. You annoy us by not doing so, by trying to reinforce to us that you are a person and not an appliance. Should you take it a step further and then attack the very pieces of technology that we love and rely on you can expect a horrendous response from us.

## 34 Expect Us to View the World the Way You Do

As an empathic person we know you have a worldview that many people regard as healthy and laudable. You are the caregivers and the healers and you feel an obligation to try and heal the world. You have an indefatigable belief that everyone can be helped, that with the correct assistance and guidance any problem can be surmounted. It may take time, it will take effort and sometimes it requires money but there is a solution. You are optimistic and a firm believer in hope. The world needs people like you (if only to feed people like us). You are giving and believe other people can do this as well. In fact, this trait of your invariably leads you to disadvantage but you do not mind this. You accept that as part of your role there will be times when your loving nature will not be reciprocated, that the money you lent someone may not be repaid or the help you provided may not always be returned. You are content with this state of affairs. Such is your balanced outlook you do not expect everyone to be like you. You recognise and cherish differences in people, but you do think that people have shades of what you possess. Some may possess more of your abilities and other less but it is there in everyone. It is not with us.

You consider the world a marvellous and fascinating place, which is bristling with opportunities to learn, grow and help. It is full of adventures and a place where we can all do well. One act of kindness each day will go a long way. You expect everyone to at least knowledge that.

You consider this to be a universal truth. Even people who do bad things can be persuaded to change given the right love and support. Redemption is available to them. You regard the world a place where if you give you will receive, what you put in you will get backing spade loads and it is an opportunity to shine. You put great stock in the fact that you do not need to blow somebody else's light out to make your shine brighter.

When you become entangled with us you think that we should be able to see what you see. All we need is to be given time and help. You are willing to do this, to exhibit great patience in attempting to understand us, guiding us and aiding us as you are intent on fixing us. You truly believe we can, with your help, see the world the way in which you do. We have heard you say it many times and repeatedly you have espoused the joys of looking at the world in the way you do.

We do not see the world in the same way as you and neither can we ever do so. The world to us is black and white. You are either with us or against. Everyone is to be used for the furtherance of our need to acquire our fuel. You will either do what we want, submit to our control and provide fuel or you resist doing so and you have to be persuaded or discarded. We see threat everywhere we go. People are trying to dislodge us from our special perch because they are jealous of our successes. They want what we have and since there is not enough of it to go around they will try and steal it from us. We must remain on guard for those who seek to undermine and depose us. We remain wary of the enemy that wishes to destroy our carefully constructed myriad of appearances. They plot to free what lurks underneath and we must not allow that. We do not want to even contemplate that which waits to be unleashed and therefore those that stand in our way must be move aside or be crushed. It is nothing personal because we do not consider individuality when we deal with people. You are either going to provide us with fuel, not provide us with fuel or try and steal our fuel. That is how we look at the world.

We embrace those who provide fuel. They are what we want. We concentrate on drawing you in, sucking you dry, pushing you away and then letting you build up the supply of fuel once more before we pull you back in again. Those who do not provide us with fuel, either because they know what we are and avoid us (rare but it does happen) or they are not the type of person who is designed to provide us with what we need, are ignored. They serve no purpose to us and therefore we have no interest in those people. The dangerous group are those that seek to steal our fuel. These people must be crushed. These people try to steer those of you who give us fuel, away from us. You warn people about our behaviours. You try and prise away our fragments and shards to allow what lurk beneath to escape. You goad and pull at our masks, trying to wrench them free. You interfere with our supply lines, seeking to cut them and switch them off and you are very much our enemies.

It is usually the case that those who become our enemies were once those who supplied us. They have learned what we are. There are those who gain knowledge who seek refuge as they recover and have nothing more to do with us as they apply the principles of no contact. These people pose a challenge and we may pursue them for a time in the hope of extracting some further fuel from them, this fuel being all the sweeter for having been denied to us. Others decide that they will fight back and turn others away from us, warn people about our behaviours and try and bring our edifice crashing down. We must destroy those people.

Accordingly, our worldview is rather simple. Are you fuel or not? Are you trying to disrupt our supply of fuel? That is all we care about. We do not see a world of opportunities to better ourselves, help people and "make a difference". We see appliances wandering around waiting to be attached to us and we must dedicate our lies to achieving this. Anything we might do such as entertain people, invent things, create marvellous pieces of art and the like is entirely incidental. All that those things amount to is a variety of methods of acquiring the fuel that we want. We do not set out to entertain a huge crowd because we like to entertain people; we do it because we receive a massive supply of fuel from people admiring what we do when we perform.

We cannot look at the world in the way you do because that means we become distracted from gathering fuel. Any distraction means we have less time and energy available to harvest fuel. A reduction in fuel risks that the tower we have constructed and that we must maintain, our myriad of reflecting shards may begin to fall about and thus that which waits beneath will be freed. That must not happen. We cannot be like you and we cannot look at the world in the same way. Do not expect us to do so, it will only end in disappointment, frustration and hurt for you.

## 35 Second Guess

We want and demand that you spend your time trying to second-guess what we will say and do. This makes us feel powerful and omniscient and at the same time it will exhaust you and leave you unable to cope. This lessens the risk that you will find the strength to try to leave us and remove that supply which we hold so dear.

Through the application of our manipulative techniques we push you into a position where you are left having to ascertain what we might do in order to please us and most of all to try to escape our wrath. This is a near constant state of vigilance where you are treading on eggshells as you try to negotiate your way through another day. It is hard. It is unpredictable. It is designed to condition you to our way of thinking so that you keep on supplying us. It is a method of control and it is utterly damaging to you.

We enjoy you trying to second-guess what we do so much because it makes us feel like a god. Before you do anything you must consider whether it will please or annoy us. It also strips you of your identity. You no longer think for yourself but you have to change your thinking to consider what we want. I wrote above how you can never make us see the world in the way that you do. Not only will we not change so that can be achieved, we will alter the way you look at the world. We force you to regard the world through our eyes. Your decisions are no longer your own as everything must be considered against our matrix. You become our attachment, your self-esteem melts away and you become our appliance.

We regard getting you to this position as the pinnacle of achievement. You have become an automaton that is geared to establishing what our needs are and fulfilling them. Should you not do so then you will suffer the consequences by being subjected to one of our vicious rages.

The problem you face is that we cannot be completely second-guessed because we keep changing the rules and the circumstances. I have written elsewhere how some people regard being ensnared by a narcissist as being trapped in some kind of prison. It is worse than that. In prison there are rules and conventions which if obeyed means that your period of incarceration will pass quicker and without incident. Stand in that place, be quiet at this time, and do not look at him. Rules both formal and informal to be adhered to so that you do not feel the wrath of prisoner or prisoner guard. There are no such rules when we trap you. It is akin to being in a concentration camp where as the camp commandant we can do as we please, whenever we please and in what ever manner suits us and you have no way of knowing whether the next thing that you will do will lead to you being shot. The way we change our minds and our behaviours, so that last week we liked a particular food but now we do not want to eat it makes your life extremely difficult. Not only is this random nature difficult to address, when you fail to do as required (and you will) you are punished with blistering fury at your failure to appreciate us and give us what we want. You are expected to know at all times what we will want and need, even if it changes at a moment's notice.

Someone who is subjected to his for long periods will be made ill. The hyper vigilance combined with the erratic behaviour and repeated chastisement will take its toll on you. Trying to second-guess us is exhausting and ultimately futile. Yes, we want it but the cost to you of doing this will be substantial. You lose your identity and your sense of self. You are exhausted and anxious from being a state of high alertness nearly all the time. You feel unsettled and jumpy. You forget who you are and the concept of relaxation has become alien to you. You are treated horrendously being insulted and shouted at when all you have tried to do is the right thing. Subjected to this for any length of time will result in a major breakdown for you.

Do not fall into the trap of trying to second-guess us. You may like to please, it is in your nature, but this is trying to please someone who can never be pleased. You are condemning yourself to a form of slavery and ultimately illness.

# 36 Share Passwords

We aim to achieve total hegemonic control of you. As I have just written, when we have you attempting to second-guess us then we know we have achieved it. In order to bring about this state of affairs we must know everything about you. My kind of course apply a ruthless approach to learning much about you in order to seduce you at the outset but we always need more information. We must acquire more knowledge about you. This is not so we can try and please you. No, the seduction is long over. This is about finding out information that we can use against you, securing knowledge that we can twist to suit our own warped agendas. We want to know where you, what you are doing and what is being said. The most effective way we achieve this is to obtain your passwords from you. There are several key passwords that we require: -

1.    For your smart phone;

2.    For your social media accounts;

3.    For your e-mails;

4.    For your PC, laptop or tablet

5.    For your bank

We will always seek to acquire this information during the golden period. Your defences have been lowered as you bask in the radiant sunshine that pours from our every smile and gesture.

We will ask you to provide us with your passwords and pass codes on the basis of being caring. What if for example you fell unconscious and we needed to call one of your friends or a family member, how could we if are unable to access your contacts? We may need to attend to your finances if you happened to be hospitalised so it would be advisable to let us know what the password is and the other information that is required to gain access. Similarly, what if I need to use the computer when you are out and mine is not working, or I need to access an e-mail for you? I only need the password for emergency purposes, honest.

You may be amazed at how often people will freely provide this information to us. They are bedazzled and feel they can completely trust us and thus they hand this information over. If we meet with any resistance, we will talk about how it will bring us closer together and show just how much you really do love and trust us by letting us have this information. We usually get the passwords.

Should you refuse to do this then we will have to resort to alternative means to cause you to share this information with us. We are unlikely to be able to get every password from a different technique but what this does is provide us with greater leverage to cause you to share. We always start with your smart phone.

Obtaining your phone pass code is easy as we just watch what you tap into it when you are sat next to us. Alternatively, we will look at where the fingerprints are and then try the various combinations of where the marks are until it works. Our brilliant memory will store that information for when we use it. We will then use it to our advantage by not just having a look through your contacts, your emails and text messages that are stored on your 'phone. We will sift through your photographs and videos along with your calendar. It is highly likely that the number you use for your pass code for your phone will be the same for your tablet so we are in there as well. This trawl through your personal information is purely done because we have to know. It is what we do next that is the real purpose of having accessed your phone.

Best of all however is the fact that we will choose a moment when you are in the shower or asleep to access your phone and download software onto it so that we are then able to access your 'phone remotely. Having to sneak repeatedly to check through your 'phone is the mark of the amateur. We will download this software, which will then enable us to monitor everything you do. This will give us access to most, if not all of your information and thus we can keep an eye on what you are up to without you knowing. We will of course use the information gleaned to bolster our abuse of you.

If we find that access to your phone is not providing us with all the information we need, then we need to obtain some leverage to gain the other passwords. To do this, we will use the software we have applied to your phone to send a message on your behalf to other people. Imagine the carnage that this will cause? We will later challenge you about this behaviour and you will naturally deny what you have done. We ask to see the evidence and you unlock your phone and go to your sent messages only to find the offending text sat there.

On so many occasions you have attacked us and brandished electronic proof about our misdemeanours. Now the tables have been turned and we are relentless in demanding that you provide us with other passwords so we can check that nothing untoward is going on. We will rant and rage at you until you provide them to us. You will do it so that we then have access to everything. If you try and change the passwords we will accuse you of deceit and demand their provision.

With total access we may have lost the element of observing you whilst you were oblivious but now we have you on edge because you know you are being watched. Moreover, we will still find something innocent that you have sent in a message of posted on a social media site and twist it so that it can be used against you.

With access to your bank information we will use this to our advantage by utilising your resources to further our aims, by transferring money (and spending it on either ourselves or fresh prospects) or taking out loans in your name.

When we are about to discard you we will use our access to turn friends against you, engage in smear campaigns and character assassinations and wreak havoc. Nude photographs that we begged you to submit to will be posted and all from your accounts and nothing to do with us.

Sharing your passwords with us is something we aim to secure. Do not do it, no matter how well intentioned we sound as we will only use them against you. Be guarded when accessing your phone and email, do not give us any clues or divulge this information to us. You will come to regret doing so if you do.

## 37 Expect Credit

This section is primarily concerned with business and work. As I have explained above, we are creatures of economy and prefer for other people to do the legwork. This also means that we like other people to come up with the brilliant, new idea and thus we are then in a position to take the credit for that idea ourselves. We are magpies. If something shiny and sparkling is put in front of us, we will happily snatch it and claim that it belongs to us.

If you find that you are working with one of my kind, any kind of novel proposal, good idea or money-saving scheme that you may think of will be appropriated by me. You work for me and therefore I regard it as your obligation to do things, which make me look good. Moreover, if it were not for the marvellous way that I have trained you, you would not have the skill set or ability to think of this point. In reality, I created it and allowed you to nurture it before returning it to me. You are not really equipped to have the big ideas, I have furnished you with the ability to generate something, which needs to be relayed to me so that I can finesse it and then present it as mine. I gain the credit and you gain the reward of not being subjected to one of my withering tirades against your competence and commitment.

My kind is especially apt at doing this with their children. We do not praise them for their accomplishments but instead gain power by claiming their achievement is down to us. It gives us fuel in a vicarious fashion. Our child has performed excellently in examinations and rather than congratulating him or her on their performance, we proclaim that their cerebral excellence is all down to us.

"He gets his brains from me."

"She did so well because I taught her the value of hard work."

"It was my revision techniques that helped him secure those grades."

People remark how proud we must be of these accomplishments and this admiration creates fuel for us.

How many times do you hear of certain people accused of plagiarism? They took a particular riff from a less well-known song and turned it into a huge hit? An idea for a screenplay was purloined by a famous director and became box office gold? That is our kind at work. Once we have rightly taken our place in the stratosphere of the special it becomes easier to steal the credit. People less well known will appear with their ideas and suggestions and offer them to us for consideration. We will reject them and then use them ourselves but pass them off as our creation. Try and sue us and we will mobilise our resources to head you off at the pass. We will deploy our manipulative skills to ensure you are regarding as a troublemaker. You have been stalking us and are no more than an obsessive fan. You pinched the idea from us and then tried to make out that it was yours.

Taking the credit for your ideas works best for us in the world of work and business because there are more people who will then praise us for our false achievement. This greater number of admirers gives us more fuel and makes us feel more powerful. It also helps to support our carefully constructed persona of successful businessman, talented musician or outstanding artist. This need for repeated admiration will bleed into our home lives as well. Should you select a gift for a family member, by way of example, which exhibits that some care and thought has gone into it, when that person opens it and declares their surprise and thanks we will step in and tell them how hard we look for it so that their thanks and admiration shines on to us. If you dare to contradict us by pointing out that it was you who selected, the gift (and since when did we ever bother to think about buying anybody else something?) then expect to be attacked. Our behaviour in this regard can be regarded as petty. We return home to see that you have spent the entire day painting the living room.

"It was a good colour I picked, wasn't it?" I will remark without any hint of shame as we ignore your hard work and seek to steal the credit for a job well done. If one of our children has done a good job cleaning the car and you make mention of this, I will dive in by stating,

"Yes but I showed her what to do."

Not only must I claim credit for anything and everything, nobody else is allowed a look in. The spotlight of congratulation cannot ever shine on anyone but me. Do not expect to be thanked or given praise for what you do for us or around our home. I expect you to do this and after all, I earn the money that pays the mortgage so the least you can do is run a decent home in return. This repeated need to seize the glory and deny you even a modicum of thanks and credit becomes infuriating and underlines our child-like need for repeated praise and admiration.

## 38 Expect Originality

You may have worked out by now that we lack originality. We like to think that we are different but our kind is all much of a muchness. We view the world in the same way, we interact with it in the same way and we do and say the same things, over and over again. Wake. Fuel. Sleep. Repeat. Was it not for the fact that when you cut us we bleed you would mistake us for being a machine.

We are programmed do to one thing and one thing alone. Obtain fuel. The path of least resistance is the one that is the most attractive to us. This consists of seducing you; devaluing you and discarding you, before hoovering you back in once again. All of my kind does it. There will be variations on the theme but the modus operandi are the same for us all. Do read **Evil** and **From the Mouth of a Narcissist** and you will see the same sayings and behaviours detailed there. Our kind is easy to predict once you know what we are. It is bizarre in a way. We are the masters of disguise and chameleon-like in our behaviour, yet we always do and say the same things. Narcissists are always very similar in their words and actions. Should you ever be in a position to compare notes with someone else who has done the dance with the narcissist you will realise that everything that has happened to you will have, most likely, happened to them. Of course, there are variations in the extent of the behaviours. This is where there are some differences. Some of our kind use physical violence to further their aims, but I do not. Others are obsessed with the body and others the mind. Bar those differences, everything else is similar. The same declarations of love, the over bearing yet somehow sweet behaviour, the switching in behaviour and the manipulative techniques that are deployed as you are devalued and the ultimately cast aside. We then do the same again as we pick you up and seek to squeeze more fuel from you.

Do not expect us to do anything that is original with you. The songs we say that are out songs were trotted out to our last conquest and they will form the basis of our seduction of our victim after you. The places we took you to and made them feel marvellous for you are tried and tested by the dozens of others who have been on the receiving end of our largesse. All of the comments, whispers and compliments have been said thousands of times before.

"I have never felt like this before."

Except for last week. Oh and the week before that. And the week before that. You will be fooled by it every time. There is a reason you fall for it. We know that it works so brilliantly because we have used it so many times in the past. We will keep on using it too because there are so many people who have no idea about us and the methods that we use.

Remember, you are not special. We are the special ones. We do not see you as an individual. You are an appliance to provide us with fuel and all appliances will be treated in the same way because that is how the fuel is given to us.

We behave in the same way as one another because you are all the same to us. Your name is meaningless to us, the nature of your childhood only relevant in so far as it provides us with material by which we can attack you later and your interests and hobbies only matter when we are finding things to talk about with you when we are seducing you. After that we strip away what makes you the person you are, because those features are extraneous to us. They serve no purpose after the initial seduction and as a consequence they can be disposed of. Every time we want you as the same malleable appliance so that our actions can be deployed in the same way. This minimises effort and ensures that we get our fuel. Our lack of originality stems from our love of efficiency.

You can use this lack of originality to your advantage. By being aware about the similar methods by which we act, once you have identified a narcissist you will easily spot our kind again. The camouflage peels away and the subterfuge fails. We will not later our approach because it is efficient. If you are lucky enough to detect us at an early stage, we will simply shrug and look elsewhere. You managed to escape as a consequence of our lack of originality, but there is always another victim who will fall for it.

# 39 Deny What Is in Front of You

This section links with listening to your gut instinct, which was mentioned much earlier on. When we are subjecting you to our manipulation and our horrible treatment of you during the devaluation you will regularly say to yourself,

"This is so horrible, why is this happening?"

"This is abusive behaviour, why does he do it to me?"

"I cannot stand how she treats me. What have I done wrong?"

"This is disgusting. What have I done to deserve this?"

You recognise that you are being ill-treated. You are alive to the fact that you are suffering abuse yet you will still deny the reality of it. You do this for two reasons. The first goes back to the type of person that you are. As an empathic individual you will always reflect and consider whether you have any part to blame in bringing about this situation. That is not to suggest that you are actually to blame for the way you are being treated. Not at all. That is entirely our doing. The point I am making is that you are prone to consider if you have any culpability. You will also try and see the good in people, as you do believe that all people have goodness inside them and it just needs to be found. People do bad things because bad things happened to them and they do not know any different. That is the view that you take. This may work with other people but not with us.

The second reason you accept this behaviour is because we have been successful in drawing you into our fantasy land. Here you know that you feel unhappy (heaven knows we have heard you say it often enough) and that the feeling of anxiety is ever present. You may wonder what it is you have done to be treated in this manner because of your penchant for introspection. You are also made to wonder in this manner because we repeatedly reinforce to you that it is your fault. We twist and alter the reality to make you the blame for everything. By telling you this over and over again you start to believe. You are weakened and exhausted so your ability to cope has been eroded. Our savage words fall against you like hammer blows, driving the concept into you that our rage, our anger and our fury has once more been caused by you.

"If you really loved me then you would not make me angry."

"How many times have I told you not to question me?"

"If you weren't so pathetic I wouldn't lose my temper with you."

"Don't be sorry, be accurate."

The cruel remarks are calculated to make you believe that it is your fault.

The intermittent glimpses of heaven that we provide to you also serve to cause you to deny what is really happening to you. The occasional days where everything feels wonderful again is our device to keep you hanging in there. It also enables us to make you think that we are a good and loving person really and that it is something else that causes to be cruel and caustic towards you. You try to fathom out what that indefinable nothing actually is in your fruitless quest to try and fix us. You are made to think that once again it must be you that is causing it. We show you how fantastic we can be and this makes you want it all the more. That is the whole purpose of that behaviour. It makes you deny reality in your pursuit of the unobtainable. We dangle the reward in front of you and this is stunning in its ability to make you endure all manner of awful treatment and deny that it is us that it is behind it.

"He isn't that bad all the time, sometimes he is really sweet."

"He can be so wonderful; I guess I just need to give him a chance."

"There are times when she sweeps me off my feet. It makes all of the horror worth putting up with."

Our behaviour hides in plain sight. We are abusing you yet you will continue to deny that we are the architects of this because of: -


1.    Your tendency to self-analyse and blame yourself;

2.    The reinforced nature of our blame labelling; and

3.    The intermittent golden period we let show again.

You must see beyond these devices. You recognise that you are being hurt and abused. You must not deny what you see. What you see is we doling out this horrible behaviour to you. Admit it.

## 40 Expect Us to Accept Responsibility

There is a popular quote about the relationship between ascendancy and obligation.

"With great power comes great responsibility."

Interestingly, the origins of this well-known quotation are not entirely clear. Some attribute it to Voltaire and others claim that it arose from the Spider Man comic book. Leaders have made use of the phrase as well, from Lord Melbourne, Winston Churchill, Teddy Roosevelt through to Franklin D. Roosevelt. It matters not where this quotation arose from but it is well recognised.

We want and wield great power but the last thing that we ever want is responsibility. Responsibility denotes accountability, which means accepting blame, and we never do that. Our huge sense of entitlement means that we must be free to come and go as we please and be able to act free from any constraint. The shackles that are associated with being responsible will interfere in our search for fuel. The energy that is taken up in dealing with a situation that we have created means we have less energy to use to obtain that fuel. Those are not situations that we can countenance.

We do not accept that we can ever be to blame and therefore we will not accept responsibility. We like to cause chaos and carnage and drink deep on the emotional reactions that our behaviour creates. We will hurl a metaphorical hand grenade into a situation and then walk away whistling as it explodes.

You become dismayed and even annoyed by our repeated inability to conduct ourselves in an appropriate way so that we accept the responsibility for the things that we do. You hold integrity high as a valued trait. You take responsibility for your actions and you therefore expect other people to do the same. You expect us to do the same. It seems entirely logical to you that if we have caused a problem then it is our responsibility to sort it out. We disregard this completely. We do because we are superior and we are above being held to account. We also know that because you are full to the brim with integrity that you will step in and tidy up the mess that we have left behind. You do this from a sense of obligation and also foolishly in the mistaken belief that we might see what you are doing and learn from you taking this action.

If our behaviour has hurt and offended others, you will feel a sense of responsibility arising from your connection with us to remedy the problem. We are also fully aware that if our conduct has caused you hurt and you wish to blame us, we know that you will try and lecture us on our responsibilities in another fruitless attempt to make us see the error of ways. I am sure you can work out by now what this lecturing amounts to? Yes, another dollop of fuel for us to savour.

When you point out what we have done wrong we will not accept it. Instead we will go on the attack and identify an area where you have failed to take responsibility in some way. If this has happened, we will remember and use it and if somehow it has not we will invent some supposed lapse on your part. This accusation will offend you as you pride yourself on your integrity. You hold dear your acceptance of responsibility and for anyone else to suggest to the contrary mortally offends you. We know this and we know that you will react to this criticism with protest and emotion. Not only will you fall for our ruse of shifting topic so that your original complaint about us is lost, you will also react in a way that gives us even more fuel. This sets in train a fantastic way for us to get additional fuel in the following way: -

1.     We do something, which causes a problem;

2.     We do not accept responsibility for that act;

3.     You point out to us the error and blame us;

4.     We deny the blame and attack your integrity instead;

5.     You react to this;

6.     You regard this attack as unwarranted but further evidence of our complete inability to be accountable;

7.     This causes you try harder to make us accountable;

8.     This gives us more fuel;

9.     You are indignant at our intransigence as you try and force us to accept responsibility; and

10.    This gives us more fuel

On and on this goes and all the while we are drinking deep as you supply us. We have no concept of responsibility and we will do out utmost to evade being held to account. You will only become frustrated in your attempts to persuade us to be responsible as once more you pick up the pieces on our behalf and continue to give us the fuel we crave.

# 41 Get Angry

This is a straightforward thing you should not do with our kind. You know we treasure emotional reactions as they provide us with fuel. Anger is one of our favourite reactions to obtain from you. We will push you and push you in the hope that you will snap and erupt into a fury. Unlike anybody normal, we do not mind being shouted at. We do not have a problem with someone engaging in a lengthy and heated diatribe against us. We want it. It is attention. Many people can understand how we love to be admired and adored since people do like to be seen in a favourable light and they accept some people may want more of it than others. What a lot of people do not grasp is how our kind revels in a negative emotion being displayed towards us. The shouting and the harsh words do not hurt us because we know we are superior to you and the fact that you are providing us with fuel means that our superiority is reinforced. You think that you are giving us a dressing down when all you are doing is giving us the very thing that we need. Who is the fool now eh?

By getting you angry we achieve the following: -

1.      Fuel;

2.      A collection of comments and behaviours from you that we can throw back you on the next occasion. "How dare you shout at me," "Did you hear the way you went on?" "You need some kind of help with your temper".

3.    It reinforces our superiority;

4.    It confirms to us that you are weak by indulging in this behaviour;

5.    It provides us with material to go to other people with and point out how unreasonable we have behaved, so that they believe us and not you in the future. We were calm and collected whilst you lost your head.

6.    We know you will feel guilty for having lost your temper. You do not usually regard shouting as an effective way of communicating with someone or resolving a dispute. You have said that to us so many times previously when we have unleashed our anger against you. You feel that you have let yourself down and you will feel obliged to apologise to us. That makes us feel powerful.

7.    You will blame yourself for the poor outcome. "I should have kept my temper", "I cannot believe I went off it in the way I did." What you fail to realise that it was not your fault. It has been out systematic abuse of you over time that has caused you to explode in this fashion. Yet again, being overly critical of yourself, you will chalk the loss of control down to you and not to us.

8.    It allows us to play the victim card if we wish. This will result in an immediate sense of guilt on your part and the empathic part of you will rush to soothe and support us with you apologising over and over again. Yes, it is yet more fuel.

9.    If the anger is particularly heated we may respond in kind and worse. We will use your anger as an excuse for our unacceptable behaviour. We may have hit you by way of response and rather than

apologise for such conduct we will attribute it to you and your temper. In line with your own personal traits and our conditioning of you, you will accept the blame for this.

There is nothing to be gained in you becoming angry with us. You will not solve anything and all you will do is play into our hands by giving us a selection of additional methods to attack you and make you feel bad.

## 42 Think We Know Everything

We like to maintain that we are the font of all knowledge. This chimes with our innate sense of superiority and our god-like qualities. We know more than anybody else on a particular subject and we have no hesitation in letting everyone know that. If we go to a party and engage in a conversation with a doctor, we will demonstrate we know more than her about medicine. Usually the recipient of this treatment is too polite to do anything about it and lets us have our moment. This suits us just fine. We have an audience as we show off. If we retain a lawyer, we start to tell him about the legal system and how the court case should be presented. After all, we have watched some legal dramas and we once escaped a parking ticket so we are regular Atticus Finches when it comes to matters of a legal nature. You are an art critic, now listen to me regale you with tales of the marvellous pictures I have seen. You play football? How about I tell you about how good I was and here are some of my suggestions for improving the game.

How is it that we behave in this manner? As mentioned, we are special and superior and we do know more than everyone else. We are experts at clothing ourselves in the parts of others and passing that off as the whole. Similarly, with knowledge we are able to pick up sections of information and knowledge and then use that to appear like some polymath with a huge and deep understanding of any subject you care to mention. We also like to maintain control in a conversation. If you demonstrate that you are more knowledgeable than us, this asserts that you are better than us and this will make us inferior. That cannot happen. We must get in first and show that we are the ones with the greater intellect.

Of course we do have considerable ability to begin with. Many of our kind are the type of people who are naturally bright and intelligent but we decide to apply this cerebral advantage to the dark arts of boast and belittlement, rather than to any greater good.

We love nothing more than listening to somebody saying something and then pointing out that they are actually wrong. The look on their face is to be treasured, as they are so crestfallen. This generates more fuel for us as they try and argue against us and especially if we have a number of onlookers. We are not ones to back down from an argument and we relish the opportunity to lecture somebody else.

Behind this front of being all knowing lays very little substance. It is similar to the way that when we seduced you, you found out what you liked and pretended to like the same and be an expert in the field. If you pressed us about how often we, for example rode horses and had we done so competitively, where and what did we win, what events did we compete in and such like you would have found us changing subjects or taking refuge in the vague. Question us closely on something and you will find us wanting. Of course, we will not take this lying down and we will use our skill at manipulation with a healthy layer of charm to try and rescue the situation since we cannot be seen to lose face. A continued close examination of our credentials in this field or some choice questions about esoteric matters will soon have us slinking away or looking to talk about something else. It takes some time, as we will not relinquish the limelight easily. This will enable you to show that we do not know everything and as a consequence you should not think that we do. We like to portray this since not only does it make us look good and it reinforces our superiority it has you placed on the back foot. We place great stock in the adage that every battle was won before it was ever fought and by engaging in a display of massive intelligence and knowledge we hope to have you thinking that you will pale in comparison to us. You will give up before even making an effort to try and argue against us or prove us wrong. Look how massive our intellect is. We have a brain the size of a Canada. By reminding yourself that we do not know everything you will not be adopting a supine position from the beginning and you will feel stronger. Our brain may indeed by like Canada; frozen and to a large extent mainly empty.

# 43 Expect Us to Listen

Our kind is the worst at listening. There are several reasons why this is the case.

1.    What we have to say is always more important than anything else that someone else might have to say;

2.    You have nothing of interest to say;

3.    When we listen we have to give you or someone else attention. That is of no use to us.

4.    We need fuel, that means we need attention and thus we need people to paying attention to what we are saying;

5.    We do not often actually hear what you are saying because we have a pre-conceived notion of what your words mean to us. This notion will be different to the one you attach to what you are saying;

6.    We are too busy thinking about what we are going to say next that makes us look good;

7.    We are too busy thinking about what we are going to say next to make you look bad;

8.    We are plotting our schemes for finding more fuel and this occupies us to the exclusion of everything else.

Next time you are talking to one of our kind pay close attention to our expression. You will see that we have glazed over. We have tuned out what you are saying because we have absolutely no interest in what you have to say unless you are talking about us, praising us or admiring us. We dismiss all of the other topics, which form the oil that eases the wheels of social interaction. Why would we want to know how your day at work has been? It does nothing for us. We are not interested in your opinion on a political matter, what do you know about it? We are the authority on that particular issue. So what if your mother has had a fall, what do you want me to do about it? It has happened, you deal with it.

It is perhaps when we are required to listen that we show just how selfish we are. We do not listen. We will talk over people, as we want to hold our place in the centre of the conversation as we dazzle everyone with our tales of brilliance and achievement. From time to time we recognise that social convention requires us to show some restraint and wait out turn to speak. We will do this but we will not listen. We will be thinking about all the fantastic things we can talk about that demonstrate out exaggerated accomplishments, the savage put downs we will be able to deploy in order to wound you or someone else who threatens to steal the limelight.

As usual this is driven by our hunger for fuel. When we are forced into silence and have to listen to someone else then we are begin deprived of fuel. How long will this state go on for? Will it last long? I can feel the tremble of the edifice beginning to shake as this loss of power starts to threaten my creation. I am sure I can feel a shard peeling away. This is weakening me, I feel threatened and uncertain. I must do something.

When forced to listen for a period of time and we feel under threat we will either interrupt and start speaking again so that the spotlight returns to us and provides us with our much needed fuel or alternatively we will create some form of drama which will disappoint you as all eyes turn our way and we bask in that fuelling light once again.

You may notice us fidget and twitch when we are forced into a situation of listening. This is because our need to speak, to bring the spotlight back to us is so great that it generates in us the same behaviour as a child who knows the answer at school. We cannot sit back and know ourselves we know the answer and inwardly congratulate ourselves. That is of no use. We need the external validation and everyone must hear that we got the answer correct. We are straining, ready to commandeer control of the conversation again. It is also because we are experiencing discomfort at being made to listen to others. Our fuel is dwindling and someone else is stealing our position. We do not like it and this discomfort manifests in physical discomfort and movement.

If you expect us to listen you will once again find that you are frustrated and disappointed. IN the same way that you should not expect any support from us, you will not gain anything by thinking we are listening to what you are saying. If you ask us what we think about what you have said, we will dismiss it with a limp comment of

"Very interesting."

We will then move on to talking about what we want to and entirely disregard what might have been troubling you. Should you try and return to the point you are making we will express our annoyance that you are trying to hog the conversation. You have had your chance and said what you wanted to say; now it is our turn. We will accuse you of not caring what we have to say and only being concerned with yourself (as ever we are projecting our own behaviours on to you).

By contrast we love a good sounding board or a Horatio as I have referred to them in another publication. This arises from the play Hamlet. Horatio's role is just to be a sounding board for the Prince of Denmark as he engages in lengthy speeches. We expect this of you as well. We want you (and as many others as we can muster) to stand to one side and listen attentively to what we wish to talk about. We have no sense that we should reciprocate this and don't even think about trying to tell us that we do not ever listen to you. We are not listening.

## 44 Expect Us to Seek Treatment, Stay in Treatment or for That Treatment to Work

This is not going to happen with most of our kind. Remember that we are superior and there is nothing wrong with us, so why would we submit to some kind of treatment when there is nothing to treat? You would not go and see a dermatologist if there was no skin complaint, so why would we go and see a psychiatrist or a therapist when we do not have a disorder of the mind. Should you suggest that there is a body of people who all agree that our behaviours are beyond the normative type that society expects and that is a good reason in itself that we should seek treatment, we will not accept that. You and the lackeys whom you have recruited to try and do us down cannot possibly be in a position to judge us. We are better than you. Remember we are special. You do not know us and therefore you cannot understand us. You cannot stand in judgement. In fact, the very bias and malice that you exhibit towards us precludes you from any ability to be impartial. This is just part of your design to hurt us and deny us our fuel and we will not be subjected to your machinations. As I have written before, I am the verb, not the noun. I do, I am not done to.

Where certain members of our club do agree to some form of treatment then the outcome is unlikely to be that which you want it to be. I agreed to undergo treatment. Not because I accept that there is anything wrong with me. This is me and this is how I function. There is nothing wrong with that. I also know that it will serve no purpose other than to entertain me as I spar with the good doctors and look to draw supply from them through the games that we engage in together. No, I agreed to undertake treatment on my terms. That was in order to ensure that my liberty remains preserved and that I was not excluded from a significant sum of money. I have told those members of my family who wanted to receive treatment that it will not work but they exhibit that disturbing and quite frankly mystifying hope that some good will come of it. Does it surprise you that there are some empaths in my family?

Those of us that might agree to enter into treatment invariably only do so for our own benefit. This will be because we have engineered a situation whereby we will extract more fuel by taking this step. Alternatively, we are doing it to prevent the cessation of a source of fuel, for example by you leaving us. We do not agree to it because we want to get better. We cannot get better. We are already the best. We do not do it because we want to change. We revel in what we are and the power that we wield. Sometimes we agree as we relish the challenge that will be posed by someone trying to outwit us. It amounts to another game to us.

The treatment will invariably reach an impasse that is if we stick with it. If the particular doctor or therapist knows our kind and acts in a way that deprives us of any opportunity to showcase our talents and extract fuel from the situation, then we will become bored. We will disengage from the process and not continue with it. Should we deem that the engagement is providing us with fuel and thus we are content to continue with it, it is invariably the case that the therapist will discharge us from their care since they are unable to achieve any progress. We will no trust them as they operate to your agenda. We will not accept what they say as we know this is frame to advance your position and detract from our own. There is nothing for us to improve on, alter or change and therefore all the suggestions that are made are never going to be acted on. All we will do is regard them as a challenge to our position and react accordingly.

Often we will aim to seduce the therapist. Well, we may as well make use of the hour. This can sometimes have the desired effect if you have been stupid enough to choose someone who is not well versed in the ways and wiles of my kind. We spend our time explaining how we are the victims in all this, that we are a good person who has been persecuted by our family and subjected to their terrible behaviour. We put on such a good show (just as we did when we seduced you) that they fall for it. They may conclude that there is no issue with us or even become beholden to our charm.

If by some miracle you have identified a competent therapist or doctor who is skilled at dealing with our kind and is able to side step our manipulations the treatment will still not work. This is because for the reasons that I have advanced above we do not want to change and we cannot change.

Save your money and lessen, no, extinguish your expectations. The treatment always fails.

## 45 Settle for This Treatment

I have little doubt as an avid reader that you have also read about the experiences of other people who have become tangled in the net of the narcissist. It is not uncommon to read about those who have endured twenty years or more being abused, pushed and pulled and spun around and around. Those people who have been subjected to such a prolonged period of abuse are well known for becoming co-dependent on their abuser, developing Stockholm Syndrome and amazingly deciding that even though they know that they are being abused and they know why and that it will not change, they may as well carry on enduring it.

I know the excuses (or reasons if you wish to be more charitable) that people decide that they will remain in the grip of the narcissist. They include: -

1.     Financial concerns;

2.     Housing concerns;

3.     Children;

4.     Other dependants;

5.     Being alone;

6.     History together

7.     You feel obliged to care for me because I have a different illness

8.     Family pressure

9.     Shame

10.    Hope – you are addicted to the potential that things might get better

11.    Conditioning

12.    The intensity of my Love Bombing

13.    Fear of my reaction

14.    Denial – this is not really happening to me

15.    Pride

16.    Change is hard

17.    You want the relationship to succeed

18.    You don't mind the relationship being so lopsided because you are a giver

19.    I am broken and you want to fix me

I have written in **Escape: How to Beat the Narcissist** about the mindset you adopt and how each of these reasons is surmountable. Hopefully by reading the above you will also have realised how some of these reasons are just not credible or realistic ones for remaining in our grip.

You do not have to settle for remaining with us. Some of our brethren do become less abrasive as they age. There is a waning of energy which means that rather than be chasing after new sources of supply they become content to extract it from their nearest and dearest and possibly in lesser quantities than before. This does not ring true for all of our kind though. There are many of us who react with horror to the prospect of aging as it reminds us that we are perhaps not as potent nor as powerful as we believe. The reducing physical strength, the eroding of looks by the passage of time and the dimming of the senses can all result in a feeling of abject horror which causes us to need even more fuel in an attempt to stave off this decline. We fight hard to prevent the encroachment of age and in the same way that fuel keeps those towers climbing into the sky, it is fuel which reasserts our standing and dominance so we are able to forget about what it really before us focus on what we want to be instead. In these cases, do not expect our kind to be graceful and less fractious. Bitterness and nastiness will rise to the fore. With the advancing of age, the sources of fuel lessen and in turn the aged narcissist must lash out in an increasing fashion at those few family members and friends that remain out of some sense of misguided loyalty. Do you want to be attached to this as you enter your twilight years? The beatings may have ended but the acidic tongue, lack of support and brooding nastiness will remain intact. Is that what you want to remember as you exhale for the last time?

Those of you who are younger have the opportunity to do what you are made for and to try and help and heal the world. There are others who would benefit from your laudable traits. Are you going to remain linked to the creature, which makes your life a living hell when you still have youth and energy on your side to make good your escape? Or will you seek refuge in the familiar albeit savage and shrug and decide that this is your lot?

There are ways to free yourself from this imprisonment and even if you cannot bring yourself to take this step, there are things that you can do to ameliorate the effect of your resident narcissist. I expand on much of this in my book **Escape** and you would do well to consider its content before resigning yourself to the rest of your time on this mortal coil chained to a monster which does not care about you and will never change. You should consider the other people that might benefit from you deciding not to settle for this way of life. They might be your children, your parents, your friends and your colleagues. Do they deserve to be subjected to the whipping and stinging tendrils of our kind? Should they have to stand and watch as you slowly vanish further and further into our nightmare fallacy, the only prospect of emerging from this hell being carted out to a waiting hospital or even worse, a hearse?

There is no need for you to settle for this treatment. You have the means to do something about it. Seize those means and apply them. Don't worry about me, I will always find someone else to provide me with the fuel.

## 46 Forget that Knowledge Really is Power

The fact that you are reading this book means that you at least have an awareness of the value of knowledge. We do not like you to be knowledgeable or equipped. This suggests you might just be better than us and by now you will be fully aware that this is not something our kind likes at all. By acquiring knowledge, we fear that you might use it in some way. As Alexander Pope wrote in his *An Essay on Criticism*,

"A little learning is a dangerous thing."

We entirely agree. We prefer that you be treated as a mushroom. Kept in the dark and underneath heaps of manure. We do not want you learning about how you might tackle us, evade us or even escape us. We lose control when these dangerous ideas are formulated in your mind by your learning and acquiring knowledge. We are the holders of information, not you. We suck up all that knowledge and we do so because we know how it is to be utilised, as we always know best. Should you begin to learn how to challenge us then we face having to deploy more of our manipulative means to keep you in check. That means we have to expend more energy and that this will drain us. In turn we will be obliged to seek out more fuel and this will make this already ceaseless quest feel even harder. I do not want you knowing about the various counter techniques you can use.

You should exploit this fear of ours. Do not lose sight of the fact the obtaining knowledge gives you real power. Power to make decisions, power to take hold of your own destiny, the power to feel strong again and the power to break free from our cloying grip. Keep reading. Hunt out the many sources of information that are available to you. There are scores of books that have been written to help you identify what we are and to deal with our behaviour. Make us of these resources; read more of my writings, you are getting it from the main man in doing so. Use the Internet, blogs and forums to increase your knowledge. The more you read the more empowered you will become. It will assist you in turning the tide and causing your flickering, guttering light to grow brighter and burn fiercer. By fighting back through the use of knowledge you will strike a blow against us and in turn become stronger.

Find all the knowledge you can and absorb it. Never stop reading.

## 47 Drop Your Guard

Should you have paid heed to the last two sections and decided that you will not settle for being treated in this manner any longer and you have acquired the knowledge by which you can escape our awful clutches then should you achieve this you must not lower your guard.

It is a fact that although you may have escaped us for now we will be looking for ways to hoover you back in. This is important to us. We feel a sense of devastation once you have slipped from our grasp. We will of course pull out all our manipulative tricks by claiming we miss you, that we cannot live without you, that we are sorry and we will change. Often these work. You have dented our ego by pulling away from us. We make the decisions about when you can come and go, not you. With our pride wounded we need to teach you a lesson and obtain some compensatory fuel. The best way of achieving both of these things is to hoover you back in. If we can do this then the fuel tastes very sweet indeed and then after an initial short golden period, which we use to draw, you back and keep you we will subject you to the full horror again with something added to punish you for having the audacity to escape us in the first place. Getting you to come back to us becomes our number one aim. We want the fuel that comes with it and we want to teach you a lesson.

I need to detail the multitude of nefarious ways we will try and bring you back under our control and spell, you can learn more about that in **Escape.** We know that these methods work, as it is the case that it takes people at least seven departures and hoovers before they finally break free. That is testament to the power that we wield as we plot how to keep us in your mind and then draw you back in. We have a huge catalogue of tricks and enterprises to do this. We will apply them repeatedly and with grim determination. They will come at you from all sides. You thought the love bombing was something else; wait until you have been subjected to our hoover manoeuvre. If the suction from this behaviour could be applied to domestic cleaning, we would be billionaires.

In view of this you must never let your guard down. It is a draining consequence of the efforts we will go to to get you back, but you must apply your energies in this way. You will have recovered some strength by having broken free from our abusive stranglehold. Use this rekindled strength to fortify yourself and maintain your vigilance. We are sly and underhand and you can never switch off or we will be in there, quick as a flash, and a hook has been sunk into you or a slippery tendril has coiled about you. Use the knowledge you have acquired to maintain your defences. Utilise those that you trust to help you maintain the barriers that you must impose. Draw strength from those people. Channel everything into maintaining your guard. At first it will take considerable effort, energy and willpower but as those of our brethren realise you are not to be recaptured and will look elsewhere, you can ease up somewhat. With the more determined of my malign brothers and sisters we will test you harder and for longer to see if what you are made of. You will feel that it is never ending but there is always an end.

You must keep in mind that it would be a tragedy for you if, after all this concerted effort, you made one slip up that allowed us to gain a foothold once again and then begin our efforts from a growing position of strength to pull you back into our nightmare world. The level of effort that you will need to apply to keeping your guard up will vary over time and should ultimately diminish. The one thing you will not however be able to do is to lower it entirely. Those walls that you have built can never be knocked down. Our kind will periodically try to hoover you back in and this can take place many years after you thought the nightmare had ended. The truth of the matter, the nightmare will never end, you may be able to move yourself away from its effects but it is always there, waiting and whirling ready to suck you back in for another horrendous journey.

Once you have been subjected to the narcissist your life cannot ever be the same again. You must always remain vigilant but doing this is clearly preferable than returning to what we did to you.

# 48 Reminisce

This is a classic error, which so many people make when they have encountered our kind. You allow yourself to think back to us and when we made you feel special. This is like pressing the button to open the door, which has kept us sealed, and away from you. Once you do this you have allowed the beast back into your life. This is all it takes. You allow yourself to linger on what was once was rather than maintaining the guard, which I have explained you must keep up at all, times. Why do you reminisce and allow us back into your mind?

1.      Something has triggered your memory about us. It might be the smell of our fragrance or a particular song and this takes you back to when you had a wonderful time with us during the golden period.

2.      You feel lonely and you know that by reflecting on the good times you will feel a curious mixture of longing but also pleasure at the happy memories that return.

3.      You were curious and you wanted to find out what we were doing so you have checked on our Face book page or driven past where we live.

Once you allow that connection to be re-established you have just lit a flame next to a highly flammable material. It will ignite. You may kid yourself that a slight peek at our Facebook or Twitter profile cannot do any harm, but that is naïve. The way in which we have imprinted ourselves on your psyche through our love bombing and abuse means that you have created certain neural pathways. You have worn these grooves into your mind which means that each time you think about us the journey along this groove becomes easier and faster. The connection will always be there and even if you push the plug in, even if for the briefest of moments, you will awaken the connection. The trigger will cause a surge inside you as the memory fight to the surface once again. You may have buried it deep down in a hermetically sealed box, tripled lead-lined and seamless but you have just dug it up and flung it wide open by allowing yourself to be exposed to the thought once again. If the trigger is involuntarily, you should be of sufficient discipline to move on and away from the thought and not allow it to manifest, but the temptation to do so I strong. The memory of us wants to be cradled by you once again. If you have decided to think about us by way of points two and three above, you have breathed life into the memory again. It rises from the depths and as it does it deliberately brings with it a sense of wellness, which will grow into euphoria. This euphoric recall is dangerous because it is addictive.

You know you should not be thinking about us, but it feels good to do so. It is just a memory, yes? You can surely shut it away again? It is not as easy as this. You have opened up the neural pathway and allowed the memory to travel along it once again. The combination of the euphoric recall makes you want to think about it some more, so you. The pathway is used once again and becomes more polished, more accessible and faster. The euphoria feels so good as well and now that you have allowed that memory to reach the surface it brings with it others. You find yourself looking again at our profile; another little look is okay, surely? You locate some pictures of us together (you managed to delete the ones you had) but now you decide to copy those pictures and open a folder. The next day you have another look at them as the pathway becomes wider and deeper and there is more recall. You fondly recall our time together, reliving the golden period and the sensation of warmth grows as you keep allowing that pathway to be used. The addiction is taking hold of you and you hunt around on the Internet for more information about us. You find our work website and there is a recent picture of us in our suit. You admire how we look and remember how smart we looked when we attended that wedding with you.

All of the work that you have invested in by removing us from your life is becoming undone. It is like a breach in a dam. There is at first a slight leak, then a trickle, then a stream, then a jet and a torrent until the dam collapses. We know this is likely to happen and that is why we never believe you truly escape us. We have left enough triggers lying around in the hope that you nudge against one and this process starts.

You wonder what we are doing. You think you are over what happened to you and sufficiently strong to resist our charm a second time. Somehow the abuse does not seem as bad now and you prefer not to think about it, as you are preoccupied with savouring the wonderful feelings once again. As I have written above about salami slicing tactics, they appear here as well. Little by little you are allowing yourself to move closer and closer to us again until like a Venus flytrap we have captured you again. At first it is all of your doing. We know it will happen but we do not know that it is happening as you are the one that is opening all those boxes again allowing the trapped memories to fly high and free once more. It is addictive as you open more and more, allowing yourself to be subjected to the power of euphoric recall until you make that mistake of establishing contact with us or enabling us (often through a third party) to know you have been thinking about us. This is all we need. Once we know that we have been in your thoughts we come after you once again and deploy our seductive wiles to ensnare you. We show you we have changed and point to all the improvements we have made. It is all part of the illusion and you end up falling for it yet again. The empathy in you thinks that we deserve another chance and you convince yourself that the supposed improvements we have made are indicative of the correctness of your decision in allowing us back into your life. You have resurrected the nightmare. We do not change. Ever.

By allowing yourself to reminisce you are engaging in a dangerous behaviour, which sets in motion a chain reaction. This is something, which is only headed in one direction; the return of you to me and the resumption of your dance with the narcissist. Do not undo all of your good work. Bury those memories and ensure you bury them dead. Do not reminisce and do not breathe fresh life into them again. Should you ever find your mind wandering or a trigger has caused the thought to loom exercise your willpower to quash it straight away. To do anything other than crush the thought is to invite us to abuse you once again.

## 49 Go Back

Never ever go back to a narcissist.

No matter how much we have begged and pleaded.

No matter the heightened emotional blackmail. No matter the promises and the pledges.

No matter how wonderful it feels to be in contact with us and you feel the warmth of the golden period across your face.

No matter what we say to you, what we do and how we do it.

We created an illusion and made you fall in love with it.

We created a nightmare and we made you live it every day.

We want fuel. We want fuel. We want fuel.

You are fuel. You are fuel. You are fuel.

We lie, cheat, fabricate, deceive and mislead to obtain our fuel.

We punished you, wounded you, baited and batted you, maimed you, scarred you, terrified you and drove you to the edge of your sanity with out disgusting behaviour. We have not a shred of remorse for what we did to you. We will do it all again in our quest to secure fuel from you.

If we poured poison into a glass of water and labelled it as 'Water from the Fountain of Eternal Youth', would you drink it? Now you would not. You know that it is poison and that it will kill you despite the fancy label and appealing words.

We are no different.

We are poison. We are toxic. We are dangerous.

We are evil.

Do not go back. Ever.

# 50 Give Up Hope

We are at our journey's end. You should never give up hope when you are entangled with the narcissist. I thought I would allow some others to share their thoughts on the topic of hope.

Hope is being able to see that there is light despite all of the darkness

*Desmond Tutu*

We must accept finite disappointment but never lose infinite hope.

*Martin Luther King Jr*

Learn from yesterday, live for today, hope for tomorrow. The important thing is not to stop questioning.

*Albert Einstein*

Let your hopes, not your hurts, shape your future

*Robert H Schuller*

Three grand essentials to happiness in this life are something to do, something to love and something to hope for.

*Joseph Addison*

Hope is important because it can make the present moment less difficult to bear. If we believe that tomorrow will be better, we can bear a hardship today.

*Thich Nhat Hanh*

Hope is patience with the lamp lit.

*Tertullian*

It is a good place when all you have is hope and not expectations.

*Danny Boyle*

Hopeful thinking can get you out of your fear zone and into your appreciation zone

*Martha Beck*

You should hold onto hope. We prefer to rely on Dante Alighieri when it comes to hope.

"All hope abandon, ye who enter here!"

# Also by HG Tudor

Narcissist: Seduction

Narcissist: Ensnared

Evil

Manipulated

Confessions of a Narcissist

More Confessions of a Narcissist

From the Mouth of a Narcissist

Escape: How To Beat the Narcissist

All available on Amazon

Follow @narcissist_me

Read more at narcsite.wordpress.com

Made in the USA
Middletown, DE
09 September 2024

60658308R00126